My mother had a great deal of trouble
with me, but I think she enjoyed it.

~ Mark Twain

Introduction

STOP!

Please, be advised of my official disclaimer...

Before reading any further, you must make your way to the front of the store and proceed to the nearest checkout in an orderly fashion. Or just cut in line if necessary. Either way, you are required to purchase this book before continuing to read it!

I mean, how else am I supposed to get you to buy it?

Did it work?

You see, I've always wondered how many people actually read the introduction to a book.

Me? I usually skip over them and go right to Chapter One. But, then again, I'm not much of a book nerd.

To me—to actually write an introduction—it feels like that awkward "About Me" field of a social media site or other necessary mediums.

Stuff like...

Name: Hi, I'm Amy

Age: undisclosed

Height: short

Weight: way under for a woman of my undisclosed age

Marital Status: single

Interests: I like long "rides" on the beach (at least I think I do... I've never actually been ON a beach).

Yeah, yeah

Yada, yada

Blah, blah, blah

Awkward, right? And even more so if you write an entire manuscript about yourself! Yet, here it is, and I guess this is the introduction portion that I was told I'd have to write.

In doing so—if I've kept your attention this long—there is a God, and miracles do happen. Actually, it is true, regardless; there IS a God, and miracles DO happen!

My life is proof of that.

Though I'm still young by most people's standards—including mine—to write my up-to-now life story in autobiographical form, it has, thus far, been full of those miracles.

At times, they have been stacked two or three high.

If you're willing to take my hand and...well, if you'll come along with me, I'll share those with you as we take this literary journey together.

Along the way, we'll fling open the doors of my home, and I'll rip away the envelope of my life. You will meet my family and maybe an animal or two. (Hopefully, you'll be able to distinguish between the animals and the humans.)

If so, as an added bonus, maybe I will also introduce you to a dear friend, later on.

As we take this tour, we will discuss homemade limbs. We will talk about dogs and penguins and multicolored monkeys. We will go to school and visit Florida. We will look at tragedies and triumphs and touch on stuff of horror and things of humor. We might even try a few stunts and endure some hard knocks and soft tissue injuries. I will also throw in a speech and a few quotes to make you think I'm more intellectual than I really am.

Essentially, this book is an amalgamation of stories and events that have been the unfolding of my life as it has truly happened.

Yet, this entire project, this manuscript, my life as a whole is really about SO MUCH MORE than just me.

Come along, stick with me through the end and you'll see.

Thanks for reading!

But don't forget to make that purchase.

Table of Contents

Introduction   5

Table of Contents   9-10

Football Baby   11

Unsightly Arrival   13

A Lesson in Greek   19

Stork Reality   25

Bells of Significance   29

Old Faithful   33

Meet My MOM   37

Nurse Janet   39

Names in a Whisper   47

Meet My DAD   51

Life on Wheels   53

Early Tears   59

Miracle Dismissed   63

Baby Gifts   67

Accessories Not Included   71

Part of the Family   81

Part of Me   89

Meet the Villagers   93

Villager-I: Brooks siblings   95

Villager-II: Brooks siblings   97

Villager-III: Brooks siblings   99

Villager-IV: Brooks siblings   101

Table of Contents (cont)

Amy's Rebuttal   105

Child's Play   107

Special Olympian   115

Phantom Protection   121

Law of Motion   125

Off and Rolling   131

Halls of Learning   135

School of Hard Knocks   141

Road Shows   149

Sweet Renovations   157

Keepers of Amy   165

Girl's Best Friend   171

Shattered Glass   177

Elevated Concerns   181

Wish Trip   185

Small World   189

Of Dogs and Men   191

Crayolas and Monkey Business   197

Graduation Speech   203

Acknowledgments   211

1

Football Baby

To hear laughter and commotion coming from any part of the Brooks' home has never been anything unusual. If our walls had absorbed the amusement and chatter of the passing years, they would be thick enough with vocal insulation to resist the cold penetration of any Pennsylvania winter. The ceilings would sag with weighted humor, and the windows would rattle with persistent goofiness.

Never was it library quiet within those walls. Never was it a museum-like atmosphere. A family circus might best describe it, and the clowns were in abundance. Childish noise was a constant. In time, I became one of the culprits and as much a cause and contributor as anyone.

But there was something different in the sounds on that particular day. Attribute it to the precisely keen hearing of an extremely experienced mother. Or credit it to woman's intuition.

Who knows?

Regardless, something sounded different. Not wrong, just different. Most likely, it was the repeated calling out of football plays that had caught Mom's attention. It was coming from the sitting room. So, she went to investigate, as any mother would do if something felt or sounded a bit divergent.

There were three of us in there—my sister, Myia, her friend, Jenn, and me. According to Mom, I was about a year old at the time, maybe 18 months. That would put Myia and Jenn as being high school freshmen.

"Hut one! Hut two! Hike! Hike!"

It was Myia under center, barking the count.

Jenn was the snapper, feet spread, both hands gripping the ball.

I squirmed and giggled.

When Mom walked in she couldn't help but to laugh also, partly from nervousness and partly from the insanity of what she saw.

The ball was snapped. The play was set in motion.

Myia and Jenn roared with laughter.

I giggled hysterically. I had entered the home as a free agent and was put in the game as a number one draft pick. Yes, I was a year old, and I was playing football.

Actually, I *was* the football.

"Don't fumble her! Don't fumble her!" Mom laughed. "And whatever you do, don't spike her!"

True story.

2

Unsightly Arrival

Most babies come into the world already loved, unconditionally, sight unseen, no questions asked. They are greatly welcomed and well received. Their arrival is longed-for and joyously celebrated.

Every spontaneous sound is eagerly anticipated.

Each instinctive motion becomes involuntary art.

A yawn is admired. A sneeze is adored. A cough or a wheeze would be grounds for immediate concern.

That first cry is pleasant music to the ears of the expectant parents whose outside world becomes lost and frozen amidst a flurry of blissful activity.

Stop the presses; the details are print worthy.

Mark the time of birth.

Measure the length.

Record the weight.

Ten fingers, ten toes.

Mom and baby are healthy and well.

Mom and Dad kiss; they laugh and cry simultaneously.

Grandma and Grandpa are there, hooting and hollering without care of what anyone might think.

First-time aunts and first-time uncles cheer the good report.

Necks are hugged.

Hands clasp and shake.

Smiles are exchanged.

Cigars are passed.

All is right with the world.

It's a grand entrance, a perfect arrival.

Welcome, little one!

That's pretty much the way it happens, about 250 times a minute, every day, worldwide. It's almost as if it has been rehearsed, but it hasn't. It all just comes naturally.

There's a good chance that you were born in similar fashion. Ask your parents, if they haven't told you already. The story should get old, but for some reason, for them, it never does.

For me, it was quite different. One thing for sure, I didn't come into the world kicking and screaming. I might have had the screaming part down, but I know I didn't do any kicking because I was born without legs. I know there was no flailing of hands because I was born without arms.

Maybe it's because I was a Monday baby. You know what they say about cars that are produced on Mondays, right? It might apply to humans also. Maybe I'm an element of the whole "caveat emptor" development: "Let the buyer beware." If I had come with a warning label of any kind, it would have been that.

At any rate, this is an extremely rare condition. Babies who are born with it are usually stillborn or die from multiple organ malformations, shortly after birth. With that, I have already beaten the odds. I was born with it, and I am living with it—a life that is happy and abundant.

I consider myself blessed though I came into the world without what most babies have—limbs. And I deem myself fortunate though I came into the world with what most babies don't have—a port-wine stain.

This was a large purple birthmark that covered my entire nose and mouth area. These things are harmless but unsightly. On rare occasions, they may fade a little with time, but they never go away. Continually covering them with makeup is a person's only countermeasure.

Port-wine stain

Aside from my physical condition, there was much more that was different about my arrival. In reality, I can boldly say there was a lot that was wrong with it.

After full gestation, I arrived at 9:28 p.m. on 9/28 of the year, in Pittsburgh, Pennsylvania. My birth weight of 6 pounds, 13 ounces was considered normal for my size. But my numbers were amongst the lowest percentile.

At 14 inches, I measured a bit short on one end. Obviously I would have weighed more if I was fully developed. Without arms or legs to dissipate heat, my body temperature was slightly elevated.

Those are simply some of the facts.

These are the things that were simply wrong:

To say the lifestyle of the couple who conceived me was less than wholesome would be a grand understatement. But I'll say it and just leave it at that.

It could be that their way of living and everyday choices had an effect on their decision; one look at me after I arrived, and both turned away.

Most births are punctuated with an exclamation point. Maybe mine had a question mark. Instead of seeing a tiny baby, that's probably what they saw—a long list of questions.

Is that all there is?

Where's the rest of her?

It could have been that my entire future flashed before their eyes. It would be a dismal one for them and an uncertain one for me.

How will she eat?

How will she play?

How will she do this or that?

Apparently, I wasn't what they had signed up for. But with what I had and with what I lacked, I was all there was—their only child, their only choice. There was nothing behind door number two.

Maybe their shock turned to fear. Maybe it was all about them. Would I bruise their social status? Weigh them down? Harm their reputation?

How are we going to deal with this?

What will people say?

What will the neighbors think?

Was I a liability?

High risk?

High maintenance?

A junk bond perhaps?

Maybe I was bad stock. How could they buy long and sell short when all they were getting was short?

Did they consider me an accident waiting to happen, or one that already did?

Only God knows what they were thinking.

I'm sure they had to have asked that huge, unanswerable question consisting of only one measly one-syllable, three-letter word—*Why?*—followed by countless and varying extensions.

Why was she born this way?

Why did this happen to us?

Why…? Why…? Why…?

Strange though, for Dr. Michael Alexander, it was love at first sight. At the time, he was head of the Cerebral Palsy department of Pittsburgh Children's Hospital. He had been called in for his insight as to what should be done with me.

They say, *'One man's junk is another man's treasure.'*

It was as if I was destined for curbside pickup, and he saw value in that which others would easily discard.

Even he—a member of the non-female species, a person of the unwomanly persuasion, a man—could not fathom the notion that a woman could conceive and carry a baby for nine whole months, deliver her, and then be content to just brazenly walk away.

Had his own wife not been expecting at the time, Dr. Alexander would have gladly taken me home with him. Can you imagine the look on his wife's face if he had smuggled home a limbless, unwanted newborn inside his little black bag of doctor stuff?

Dr. Alexander tried to encourage the couple to reconsider. He attempted to coax the woman toward me, to nudge her toward motherhood. Maybe a second look would generate a second thought. Hopefully there would be a tug at her heart or at the father's soul.

There wasn't.

Not even a little bit.

It was a noble effort on Dr. Alexander's part, but there would be no second look. There was no nudging, tugging, stirring, pushing, pulling, or gravitation of any type toward parenthood.

It was that simple. Their minds were made up. They didn't want me. Not her. Not him. Not them. They walked out of the hospital without me, and they never looked back.

According to a case worker of Children Youth And Family Services (CYF), the man who would have been my grandfather offered this solution:

"Can't you just put her in a back room and not feed her?"

Also a true story.

3

A Lesson in Greek

O kay, class, take out a notepad and two sharpened No. 2 pencils. Yes, there will be a quiz at the end of the chapter.

Well, maybe there won't be a quiz, but the information might come in handy someday. What if you were to appear on *Jeopardy* or *Who Wants To Be A Millionaire*? You could end up with a boat load of cash to share with me.

Or by paying close attention, you will at least be able to impress your friends at *Trivial Pursuit* and be considered *Smarter Than A Fifth-Grader*.

Today's word is *Tetraphocomelia*.

The term is Greek (ελληνικά), an independent branch of the Indo-European family of languages.

Tetra is *four* (δ).

Phocomelia essentially means *seal limbs* (φώκη μέλεα).

Write it down. First in English, and then in Greek. Don't worry; you're not required to hold your pencil in your teeth, or between your chin and shoulder like I do.

Now, sound it out slowly: tet′ră-fō′kō-mē′lē-ă.

Try again. *Tetra-phoco-melia.*

That wasn't so bad, was it?

Now, imagine yourself in the Land of Oz. Close your eyes, click your heals three times, and say it repeatedly.

Tetra-phoco-melia.

When you put it together, it refers to having four seal limbs. That describes me, and I suppose it makes me rather unique because there are only about 150 known cases of Tetraphocomelia Syndrome in the entire world. Yet, ironically, there is a man right here in Pittsburgh who was born with it, a few years before I arrived.

He is successful, highly respected, and maintains a productive lifestyle. Nevertheless, there are two of us on the loose here.

Spooky, huh?

I will not disclose the year of my birth because a lady never reveals her age; although I'd be glad to tell you how old my mom is if you'd like. For a hearty laugh, I could also calculate it in doggie years for you.

The year I was born the global population grew to exceed 4.5 billion people. I'm counted in that figure somewhere, at least by half a person.

For those of you who know me, duck! Whether by that year's population or today's, in terms of statistical probability, you have a much greater chance of being struck by lightning than to personally know someone affected by this particular birth defect, especially with the deluxe model such as mine.

As it turns out, I have a close friend, Eric, who actually was struck by lightning.

More on that later.

Stand by for updates and analysis.

Film at eleven.

Can you imagine? I was born with Tetraphocomelia, and Eric was struck by lightning. With this combination I'm thinking the two of us should throw a few bucks together and play the Lottery.

What causes Tetraphocomelia? Frankly, there is no decisive link. Not a solitary one, anyway. There could be numerous ingredients or multiple causes.

The first medical documentation of Tetraphocomelia Syndrome dates back more than four hundred years, though the Grecian term itself wasn't officially coined until 1836.

A known fact is that Phocomelia of any variety is a gene mutation. Genetic inheritance can certainly be a contributing factor to its existence. It was also believed to be chemically induced. In fact, chemicals are believed to be the leading culprit.

One particular medicinal substance was the prime suspect.

In the 1950s, the prominent root cause of Phocomelia appeared to be Thalidomide—a German manufactured drug—which was given as a painkiller and a tranquilizer. It was also used to combat colds, coughs, and headaches, and to successfully battle insomnia.

How much would you pay for this incredible concoction?

But wait! There's more!

This one is a literal kick in the gut: Thalidomide was commonly used to fight morning sickness during pregnancy.

In those days, it was thought unlikely that any drug could transcend the placental barrier and pass from the mother to her unborn child. Clearly that was an erroneous notion. Phocomelia was then a recurring result—babies arriving with varying combinations of missing or deformed limbs.

Thalidomide was prescribed and sold in at least forty-six countries from 1957 to 1961. So, for five years there were countless expectant moms readily consuming it with a developing baby on board.

It was during that time, and in at least that many nations, when more than 10,000 children were born with severe birth defects such as Phocomelia. Many of them did not survive. More frequently affected were the upper appendages, as is the common outcome of this defect.

Babies came with fingers fused together or with one or more shrunken limbs. And then, there were the extreme cases similar to mine. These are the deluxe packages, more or less, where "more" means having less.

When Thalidomide was found to be the primary culprit, it was discontinued. But it wasn't eradicated. It remained in existence as all drugs seem to do. It just couldn't continue to be consumed like candy.

The United States Government never permitted Thalidomide for use to the extent that other nations did. In 1998, however, our Food and Drug Administration did approve it to battle Leprosum. Apparently, it's working; I haven't encountered any Lepers anywhere in Pittsburgh.

If we were to take a fieldtrip, you would find that we do possess a sufficient population of Penguins, Pirates, and Steelers that are indigenous to the area. But no Lepers.

No leprechauns either. Trust me; I'd remember if I saw a leprechaun running around.

I know you're probably wondering how we transitioned from Greek literature to Irish folklore, but try to stay focused. For those of you at the back of the class who may have dozed off, the topic is Phocomelia and how it was made popular with Thalidomide.

Essentially, the drug was taken off the shelf in 1961 and recycled in 1998. With its reintroduction in the medical field came stricter guidelines for Thalidomide because of its potential to cause birth defects.

One thing is sure: the drug was pencil-whipped a new identity. By eliminating two vowels and a consonant, it's probably more accurate to say it was eraser-whipped.

"Thalomid" became its new name.

It's like the low-cost carrier who dropped a DC-9 into the Everglades in 1996, at the cost of 110 lives. The airline immediately changed their public image by drafting a new name and designing a new logo.

New name, new logo, new perception.

The only true improvements with the Thalomid were the tighter regulations. It happened with the airline, and it happened with the medicine.

For what it's worth, in September 2012, Germany offered a public apology for the limbless babies born in the 1950s and '60s because of Thalidomide. But I suspect their words of contrition had little meaning.

Tetraphocomelia.

Four Seal Limbs.

While that basically describes my condition, it does not define me. I'll explain that later. Actually, you'll probably figure it out as I take you on this journey of my life.

So, the long and short of it (mostly the *short* of it) is this: I have two abbreviated arms. No hands.

As a fully grown adult, my right arm is seven inches in length, my left measures five inches.

I often refer to these as my *little arms*. This is not to underscore the fact that they are little, but to distinguish between those and the varied prosthetics that have been associated with my life.

Though neither of my arms has grown to elbow length, I do claim to have a left elbow. This is simply a knobby, elbow-like development at the end of the humerus bone. On a few occasions, it served well as my weapon of choice in some childish skirmishes.

Had I gone on to establish a boxing career, I likely would have been branded a south paw. In spite of its mere five-inch reach, my dreaded left cross was known to afflict great pain.

My only other source of self-defense was spitting, which I'm not proud to admit. Utilizing that resource was my equivalency of bringing a knife to a gunfight; I took saliva to a fisticuff. It wasn't very ladylike, but don't worry. I haven't had a 'spat' with anyone in a very long time.

For legs, I have none, only hips. I do refer to them as legs at times, being my nearest resemblance to such, and given the fact that I'm able to walk on them to some extent. When I do, I feel no urge to duck because I'm doing quite well at height management these days.

I haven't bumped my head in any doorways recently, and I don't expect to any time soon. Well, I have knocked and scraped my forehead many times, using the door trim to push my hair out of my eyes, but I have no overhead clearance issues.

The simple truth is that the 'up' button on my human growth elevator hasn't worked in a while. My overall height is 32 inches or about 81.3 centimeters for those of you who are into that whole metrics fad. Either way, it's a tad shy of the WNBA average. The same could be said of my vertical jump. For me to anticipate an invitation to any future Slam Dunk contests would be somewhat unrealistic.

Like others who were born with this, my specific package is different from theirs. It's a unique fit, completely custom made. I also have small appendages that would have been feet under normal developmental circumstances.

These are known as vestigial feet. They are attached at the base of my hips, and they typically don't come as a matching set.

Mine didn't.

Apparently, they are like snowflakes where no two are exactly alike.

The one on my left has two short toes that resemble pinchers, more or less. The right foot is slightly longer and has two L-shaped toes.

I am able to bear my full weight on my feet, but only for shorts periods of time. Being up on them is how I describe myself as "standing." Like most people, I also use my feet for balance.

Unlike most people, when I walk, the majority of my weight is on my bottom. But I use my feet too. I guess that would have been their original purpose after all.

As for size, with my math and measurements, one foot equals about three inches because that's about how long my feet are.

In all, it's fashion of an acquired taste. A signature look. Not everyone can pull off wearing such an outfit. I make it work the best I can.

Although the specific origin of Tetraphocomelia is unknown, mine is not without clues or suspicions.

The woman who conceived and carried me was out of the country during most of her pregnancy. Her medical care was likely far behind America's standards.

It has always been my understanding that she was given a combination of medicines to prevent a feared miscarriage, and Thalidomide may have been part of those prescriptions.

Isn't it ironic to think that a medicine prescribed to allow a woman to keep me would produce results that would cause her to not want me?

While these medicines do offer a practical and scientific explanation as to why I was born this way, no one knows for sure.

It really doesn't matter.

For me, that part is not important, even if the answer was available. I am much too busy to launch an investigation. I am living life. I am loving life. I am not in pursuit of logical answers. I am on a lifelong journey—one that is as spiritual as it is physical. I am at peace, joyful, fulfilled.

I lack nothing.

My existence, like yours, greatly exceeds material rationale. There is far more to who we are than our physical composition or outward appearance.

As for me, I move at one pace—constant.

I look in one direction—forward.

Rather than examining the past, I am focused on my future. I am not living in the womb but on Planet Earth, while traveling toward an eternal home.

It may not be widely accepted in a public classroom, but if there is anything noteworthy in today's lesson, it is this: I am a child of God, regardless.

This is an endless, unchangeable truth, and there is absolutely nothing Greek about it.

As for tonight's homework assignment, please read Chapter 4 through the end of the book.

It's either that or Algebra…using the Metric System.

Class dismissed!

4

Stork Reality

I*t's a girl!*

There should have been a bouquet of pink balloons proclaiming my arrival. There should have been a sign heralding the announcement.

I should have been received, declared, trumpeted. There should have been a festive ambience, a cheerful assembly, a celebration of some kind. But there wasn't.

There was none of that.

No welcoming committee.

No merriment.

No laughter.

No glee.

I was a one-way delivery.

A one-time, take-it-or-leave-it offer.

No refunds.

No returns.

No warranty on parts or labor.

And what was there to show for it? An armless, legless, and parentless baby with a purple face. That's what the stork brought to Pittsburgh on that day. And that's what the stork and my birth parents left behind.

This was my start in life. With such an undesirable recipe, namelessness was quickly thrown in as a bonus ingredient.

But to me, the couple who was responsible for my birth was nameless also. Instead of forming that instant, magical, inseparable bond between a couple and their newborn, we became immediate and permanent strangers.

In that regard, the shared ambiguity positioned us on the same playing field; I didn't know them, they didn't know me.

Yet the advantage was clearly theirs.

They had hands, and they used them to sign the documents. They had legs, and they used them to quietly walk away—forever fading into anonymity.

I remained at the hospital, alone.

Without delay, I became a ward of the fine, friendly establishment known as the Commonwealth of Pennsylvania. Proportionally, that's a lot of state for such a little person—45,308 square miles of territory to approximately a hundred square inches of infant flesh.

Regardless, Pennsylvania born and branded, I was quickly issued a permanent social security number and a temporary name—a codename.

Admittedly, some codenames can be rather appealing and their purpose greatly significant. In certain instances it could be a privilege to need one.

For security detail only!

A high-level constituent!

Classified!

At the time of my birth, Ronald Reagan was president. He was codenamed Rawhide. First Lady, Nancy, was Rainbow. Are those awesome codenames or what?

Theirs was assigned for precautionary reasons, for protective measures, for communication purposes by the Secret Service. Mine was issued for momentary identification, an alternative to referring to me as *her, she,* or *it.*

Parental abandonment is not an especially glamorous reason to be designated a codename, and mine wasn't anywhere near as cool as Rawhide or as colorful as Rainbow. Mine was just a plain, unheralded, colorless little girl name that would one day be erased. And the sooner that could happen, the better.

But how?

Well, there was only one way to lose the codename and get my life officially started. There was only one real answer. That first wrung of life's ladder for me was to be placed in a pleasant, welcoming environment where my immediate needs could be met. From there the eventual and most hopeful outcome would be permanent adoption.

What kind of person, or what type of family, would be willing to do that? Who would take a baby without limbs? Dr. Alexander probably would have, but what's to say he wasn't a rare and extreme exception?

Was there anyone else who would be so inclined?

Would anyone want a limbless baby with a purple face?

Who would care that much? Anyone?

What would happen to me?

Where would I live?

How would I survive?

Of course, I had no awareness of my situation at the time. I only ask these questions for dramatic affect. I'm going for a Hallmark movie feel. Did it work?

Dramatic or not, that was my reality. This truly was my introduction to life.

Fortunately, I was born at a very early age; I didn't comprehend the dire position I was in. I had no clue I didn't have limbs. There was no discernable indication that I didn't have parents. I held no knowledge as to who I was, where I was, or what was unfolding around me.

That basically describes the life of a newborn, I suppose. And for me especially, that was a good thing.

5

Bells of Significance

This was the famous line by Angel 2nd Class, Clarence Oddbody, to George Bailey in the 1946 Jimmy Stewart, Donna Reed Christmas classic, *It's A Wonderful Life*.:

"Every time a bell rings an angel gets his wings."

Now, replace the black and white film with vivid color. Fast-forward it thirty-five years. Crank up the volume a few decibels, with complete surround sound and lots of background noise. Mix in some additional foreground noise as well; mostly from young, rambunctious, undeveloped citizens.

The production crew has dismantled the set and has transported it south from the imaginary town of Bedford Falls, New York, to the authentic city of Pittsburgh, Pennsylvania. The Bailey home is dropped into this blue-collar land known for its work in red—seething hot steel mills and zesty Heinz ketchup.

The wintry conditions are whited out and replaced with the colors of early autumn. The flatland is covered with multiple layers of pitching landscape.

The Baileys are now the Brooks. George and Mary have been recast; Richard and Janet are now the leading roles. They are the headliners. They are the reigning stars. Together they have made a wonderful life of their own.

Inside their house, it seemed every time their telephone rang a child got a home. Some were long-term placements. Some were short-term. Most had special needs, some severe.

Rich and Janet Brooks were the "go-to" people of foster parents. Theirs was the number to call. Everyone knew it; especially the folks at the CYF of Allegheny County, Pennsylvania. If they could have had anyone on speed dial, it would have been the Brooks'.

At the time, they were a family of six, legally speaking. The kids—Brian, Candy, Myia, and Noah—outnumbered the parents, two-to-one, but it wasn't enough. Being outnumbered by children—being surrounded by babies in particular—was what this couple was all about. They would have it no other way.

Maybe it was because they had kids before they were married. Okay, that deserves some clarification. Truth is they began dating when Rich was seventeen and Janet was fifteen, and they were deeply in love.

Janet had been an only child for the majority of her childhood. When she was little, she played with baby dolls, incessantly. When she grew a little older, she sought real living babies to dote on. At family gatherings, for example, instead of playing with the other kids, she went to whoever had the babies and mothered over them.

At age thirteen, Janet became big sister and second mom to Vicki. She loved her baby sister and affectionately fought her mom to care for her. She also had two little cousins at the time, Mark and Kim, separated in age by only thirteen months.

When she and Rich began dating, they were like teen parents, having at least one toddler with them everywhere they went. If it wasn't little Vicki it was the cousins, or some child combination.

Always a "kiddie cocktail" of some sort.

They adored kids. They loved babies. And they knew they were eventually destined for parenthood together.

Janet Smith became Mrs. Richard Brooks on July 3, 1957. It was the year of an automotive icon—the classic Chevrolet Bel Air. Unforgettable car, unforgettable couple. Little did they know that they would become icons of their own. Priceless model parents, with more exquisite qualities than any fleet of extravagant vehicles.

At first glance my parents look like polar opposites. She's a perpetual chatterbox with great attention to verbal detail. He's a get-to-point kind of guy. She's lively and animated. He's a cardboard cutout.

You might even say, she's the crowing rooster, and he's the effectual snooze button. But they are identical on the inside; both are old school. So much so that Dad is the principal, and Mom is class president. That's okay because they share the same morals and values.

With them, it's what's under the hood that matters most. And it's the interior that's of highest value. That's where their greatest qualities can be found.

Though they possess great strength, it's not displayed externally like that of a muscle car. It's the fine details, not the eye-catching flash and fluff. It's their character, their faith, their overall integrity.

Long after the automobiles of that time had worn down and rusted out, this couple continued shining brightly.

Reliable.

Rust proof.

Resistant to corrosion.

They are like Robo Dad and Moto Mom, refusing to wear down. They come with no expiration date, even if not refrigerated. And as the Chevrolet Bel Air was preserved and cherished by many, so are they.

1957. He was twenty-one, she was nineteen. That's when the Brooks' homestead was established and their legacy began. Two years later they became true parents to a baby of their own, Brian. The others came along over the next fourteen years.

That's why when Noah, the youngest, turned five and started school, they decide to begin fostering. Well, Mom decided that. Dad supported it.

He was an over-the-road trucker, a steel hauler. Sometimes he was gone for two or three days at a stretch, depending on the requirements of his run. She was a stay-at-home mom, and she needed kids for which to stay at home.

She initiated the fostering idea. He agreed to it. It was a big decision, but an easy one for them to make. It was a good fit. Not necessarily an easy one, lined with fleece and sprinkled with glitter, but it was a good one, nonetheless. It was good for them, and it was especially good for the incoming babies.

The Brooks' service was offered without comfort or convenience. This was most evident by the call that actually came in one year on Christmas Eve.

It's another Christmas classic.

The Brooks were already caring for two-month-old boy/girl twins at the time, nicknamed Mickey and Minnie. Soon after the phone rang, there was another newborn delivered to the door like a last-minute Christmas package. It was like having triplets in the home.

Three little stocking stuffers.

It was Christmastime, and it was a wonderful life.

More than providers of shelter, more than caregivers, Rich and Janet Brooks were, in fact, suppliers of wings to blossoming angels.

Clarence Oddbody would be as proud of them as I am.

Listen! Their phone is about to ring once again.

Places everyone!

Quiet on the set!

6

Old Faithful

If the Brooks' ringing telephone meant a home to a child, it was likely because the home itself could have easily been dubbed "Old Faithful." The house was old, the owners and occupants were faithful.

Like the admired geyser of Yellowstone, the Brooks were known to be magnificently predictable, from day one. They were steady and reliable.

A show of beauty, a spectacular display of awe and wonder, an exhibit of natural goodness, an example of life's wholesomeness, an illustration of God's handiwork. This describes Old Faithful, and it is an equal depiction of Rich and Janet Brooks and their home.

Before and after I came along, there was a lengthy, unbroken string of foster babies there. All totaled, it was a moving conveyor that would run nonstop for twenty-five years. It would not experience any power outages. It would not be taken off line for upgrades. It would not be shut down for re-tooling; it would just keep rolling along, persistently and faithfully.

There were about twenty of them before me and more than three times that amount after. Each have a story; most are dramatic and heart wrenching.

With many, abuse and neglect was a recurring and underlying theme. One baby had been shot with a small-caliber hand gun. Another had been burned by a space heater. There was blindness, epileptic seizures, and allergic reactions to everything on the planet. The list goes on, and the challenges grew taller with each one.

Janet Brooks never said no to a request to care for a baby. Richard Brooks never said much of anything; he just remained the silent, hardworking type.

Together they make a great team. They are greatly loved. They are highly dependable. Everyone knows it, especially Linda Stewart. As a case worker for CYF, Linda handled many pre-adoption cases, and she knew the Brooks well.

When it was suggested that she call them with one particular case, Linda was hesitant. She didn't think it was a good idea or a valid consideration. Somewhere she had heard, somehow she knew: Janet only wants to take babies who are healthy.

How did she know that? Where was that memo twenty babies ago? Why was she willing to now honor that request when others had not? Was it because this was a more extreme situation than all the others?

Even after all the sickly and needy foster babies who had already come and gone from the Brooks' home, Linda didn't want to dial that particular number. In spite of the family's remarkable track record and impressive reputation, she intended to pass them by.

She realized the home was always open for business; Janet and Rich were always on duty. And it certainly was not for monetary gain. The Brooks were not "for hire."

For their tireless, all-day, every day, round-the-clock care, they were compensated an average of $6 a day—all of which went to the wellbeing of the child, at a rate of 100 % and more.

These were not wealthy folk. Not even close. Yet, they didn't foster for income. If they had, they chose the wrong profession. It wasn't easy, it wasn't convenient, and it definitely wasn't lucrative.

For them it was a ministry, a service to the community, out of love for children. Each baby was treated as if they were a Brooks. They were all well nourished, well groomed, well dressed, and sincerely loved.

To this couple, family means everything. Parenthood means everything. People are valued beyond price, especially babies and children. The home is a shelter, a safe haven, an all-out kid's zone

Old faithful.

But was this beyond the boundaries of what Janet would accept? Would this not be an unreasonable request? Was it not an irrational appeal to make? Linda could have quickly answered yes to each of these questions.

But she is a trained expert, and she realizes the need is greater than her concerns.

She takes a deep breath. Reluctantly, she picks up the telephone and dials the familiar number. The county has a baby, and the Brooks' have a good, reliable home. It's as simple as that.

Clarence is listening in. He hears the bells ring. Janet does too, and she answers.

Linda's call is professional. Business as usual, generally speaking. There was a week-old girl who needed care.

Fairly routine stuff so far.

However, there was more to the story. There was some fine print. The baby came with an asterisk and not much more. She said this newborn had no arms or legs.

Guess who that was.

Go on, take a guess.

Introduction

Meet My MOM

For now, I'd like to scoot aside and allow my parents to write these next few chapters. Without question, they are better qualified to share certain details and back-story, especially that which spans my infant and toddler years. Without them I wouldn't have a story.

First up is Mom. She's an avid reader, so she'll probably use words that she's read somewhere before. She might even throw in a few that are homemade, cooked in her own southern recipe. Be warned, Mom doesn't type as fast as I do, so you might want to read slower to keep pace.

Janet Brooks is the best mom a girl could ever want. She is giving and kindhearted, but she has a certain spunk that demands respect. Mom gets things done. She's tough but fair, and she isn't afraid to tell it like it is, when necessary.

When it comes to wit, she's hard to beat, even hard to match. She's a real blast from the past, and she takes all the credit for making me so crazy. Mom is half-baked and slightly overcooked, at the same time. If you haven't laughed until you nearly pee yourself, you haven't met my mom. If you know her, you can imagine how often I've almost peed myself because of her. Sometimes we laugh until our sides split, and then, like gluttons for punishment, we laugh some more. If you are annoyed by silliness, Mom will annoy the snot out of you.

The woman is a walking punch line, the clown princess, the court jester, and I think she's addicted to the fame and glamour that goes with it. Mom is a one-person sitcom; the childish content of which may not be suitable for mature audiences. Viewer discretion is advised.

She rarely changes the channel, and she seldom takes a commercial break.

When it comes to family and caregiving, however, she's all business, a veteran of the trade, a true professional. She takes that work as serious as anyone, if not more. You'll be reading about some of it on the following pages.

Mom is like a triple threat. She is the Mother Theresa of compassion and the Florence Nightingale of nursing. (She's not a real nurse, but she has played one in our home.) With her slender shape and her ability to keep a neat house, she also has a good percentage of Wilma Flintstone mixed in there as well.

My mom—what a gem—the perfect mom for me, the perfect mom for anyone. The woman deserves a service medal.

If she writes her chapters with a southern accent, it's because she was born in the way-down-low, in the deep-down south—about 20 miles deep, southeast of Pittsburgh.

A true hillbilly?

Yessiree, Billy-Bob!

Z

Nurse Janet

by Janet Brooks

Being from a small town a few miles south of Latrobe, Pennsylvania, I do consider myself a southerner, and I have the accent to prove it. I am from Lycippus, which is basically pronounced the same that it's spelled: Lie-Sip-Us.

The town was so named with the meaning: Some *lie*, some *sip*, and it applies to all of *us*.

I am a southern girl, but I am not a hillbilly as Amy would lead you to believe. I am more sophisticated, which makes me a hillwilliam, instead.

When I felt the urge to begin providing foster care, I prayed for guidance to do it right and for help to do it well. I also prayed for sensitivity to know when to quit—and that I'd have the strength to do it without regret or longing for the babies.

The other big request I made was, "Don't send any kids with special needs." I soon realized God has a tremendous sense of humor because He shrugged off that last part.

I do realize it might have been a bit unreasonable. I could see where one or two would eventually slip through the cracks if we fostered long enough. As it turned out, special needs babies were the only ones that God saw fit to send us.

After high school, I wanted to study nursing but changed my mind when I discovered the amount of schooling and training it involved. I didn't know that, out of necessity, I would earn an unofficial nursing degree in the classroom of parenting and through on-the-job training with foster babies.

It wasn't what I had planned; it just happened that way. In fact, if my request didn't get through to God, to not send any special needs babies, I asked the same of my foster supervisor, Doreen Walker.

I was honest about it. I was humble. I knew my limitations. I told her I didn't have any medical training. Somehow, none of it got through.

It has often been said, "Necessity is the motherhood of invention." I found this to be true as I was forced to begin practicing some inventive motherhood with these little ones—registered nursing duties included.

Our first baby came only two days after we were approved as foster parents. He was five months old, and he weighed only nine pounds. He was a failure-to-thrive baby, due to parental neglect. His mother was a single parent who often went on her way, as if she was just single. Apparently, she would forget the parent part of her categorization.

She would leave her house for hours on end, and the baby would be home alone and forgotten. When neighbors called the police, they were waiting for her when she decided to come home. Taking the baby from her saved his life.

One side of his face was flat from lying on his stomach all the time. He was cold. He wouldn't eat. He had essentially shut down. I kept him bundled up and worked hard to get him to eat. Eventually, he turned the corner.

We had him for several months, and while he improved greatly, his mother didn't improve at all. When the baby was returned to her, the arrangement only lasted about a month.

He was then sent back to our home, exhibiting all the behaviors of having been neglected and abused, all over again. This time, being older, he would head butt and scratch us when we tended to him.

He was worse with Candy, our older daughter. It was apparent that she reminded him of his mother. If I handed him to her backwards, and if she didn't speak, he was fine with her. But if he saw her face or heard her voice, he would violently slam the back of his head into her.

After a while, he was placed in a home with a family who intended to adopt him, but he was more than they could handle. He then went to a second family and was eventually adopted by them.

The most extreme case of cruelty that came our way was in the form of a battered eight-week-old girl. It was clear that she was abused from the time she was born.

Having spent two weeks in the hospital, this baby had received multiple beatings over the first six weeks of her life. The injuries were extensive and in various stages of healing. Two of her ribs were broken. Both arms were fractured. One leg was broken, as was the opposite ankle.

The baby had been shaken and her head banged against the crib. Her skull was fractured in four places near the left ear, and she had severe brain bleeds.

We had her in our home for seventeen months, initially. These many years later, Rich and I are co-parenting the girl with her mother, due to the woman's work schedule. Transitioning our dwelling from day care to schoolhouse, Amy has become the girl's learning coach. She assists her with her online classes and a variety of other educational materials.

This girl did recover from the majority of her wounds. In time they became nonexistent, as breaks and fractures and contusions eventually do. Sadly, she does bear a cognitive deficit from the brain injury, along with a few other lingering effects.

All that harm was delivered by the hands of the father; the one who is by nature the designated defender and protector. It is unfathomable that anyone could beat theirs or any child, let alone a newborn. Whatever time the man spent in prison for these actions was not nearly long enough.

The baby who was shot was also a newborn girl, sleeping in her bassinet when a handgun discharged for "unknown reasons." The bullet grazed her hip, chipping the bone. It then traveled across her stomach near her bowels and stopped without exiting, lodged just beneath the skin.

Surgery was performed on her to remove the bullet and to repair the damage. The surgical incision followed the path of the bullet, which was across her entire belly and hip. She was then placed in a body cast from her underarms to her ankles, with a small opening that would allow for diaper changes. After that, she was placed in our home.

We cared for her for about two months, while she was recovering and while her home and the shooting was being investigated by Children's Services.

To give the baby her tummy time, I wasn't able to simply place her on a quilt on the floor or in a crib on her stomach because her feet couldn't flex; they pointed straight out at all times, in the body cast. For a solution,

I sat with her as she lay on her belly, with her toes dangling over the edge of a bed.

Changing her diaper offered a different kind of challenge, but I managed to find a way to do it effectively. Each time we took her for a check-up, the doctor marveled at how clean the body cast was. I showed him how I diapered the baby without soiling the cast. He was quite impressed with my technique and said he would pass it along to his staff, should they ever be faced with such a predicament in the future.

If there is one thing I take pride in it's in the fact that, when the cast was removed, it was perfectly clean; it had no urine or feces stains, whatsoever.

In time, the baby was placed in another home, after we had tended to her and nursed her back to health during the most frightening and painful days of her very young life.

It was a miracle that, being such a tiny person, the bullet didn't hit any vital organs or major arteries. And if it had been a larger caliber or higher velocity weapon, things would have been much worse for her.

The baby who was burned was also a little girl. She was in her swing near a space heater in the home when, supposedly, her toddler brother ran by and tipped the swing. The baby fell into the heater and burned her forehead and the entire back of her hand.

Three times a day, I washed her burns with iodine solution, peeled away the dead skin, and applied ointment and fresh dressing. Eventually, her burns were determined to be an accident, and she was returned to her home.

Another baby came to us at three or four months old. When he was stable enough, ours was the first home he had entered, having spent his entire existence in the hospital. He was a crack baby, born extremely premature.

The list of his problems seemed endless. His birth weight was barely over one pound. He had holes in his brain. Twice in the hospital he had stopped breathing and had to be resuscitated. Legally blind, he had only peripheral vision. When we talked to him, we did so from the side, so he could catch a glimpse of our faces.

It was only to our voices that he showed a favorable reaction; especially when the kids spoke to him. He recognized and responded best to Myia's voice because she was around him more than the other kids were. When she would walk in and say the baby's name in three quick successions, he would smile and display some excitement. He also favored Brian's voice.

Other than that, the baby had no expression, no strength, and no motor skills. He was very weak and floppy. He was also extremely jumpy and skittish at the slightest of sounds.

When feeding him, the environment had to be completely quiet. If the telephone rang or if a dog barked outside, he would stop eating. The most he would take of a bottle was five ounces at a time, which prevented him from gaining any weight.

Every two weeks I had to take him to the hospital to be weighed and examined. His progress was literally measured in fractions. If he gained 1/4 ounce, it was good. 1/2 ounce was better. If he had gained a full ounce, they were ready to break out the party hats and celebrate. But he wasn't putting on enough weight, and he wasn't doing it fast enough.

Finally, the medical staff decided to readmit him to try to accelerate his weight gain. But with all the ambient noises and typical hospital sounds, he wouldn't eat there. As a result, he went backwards; he lost weight.

The doctor said, "We won't make that mistake again." He then sent the baby back home with us, where he did eventually put on some weight.

Regardless, the baby was always very sickly and fragile, always in and out of the hospital. He experienced breathing difficulty, pulmonary trouble, reflux problems; all because his mother had more of a desire for crack cocaine than for birthing a healthy child.

I would listen to the baby's labored breathing, and when he began wheezing I instinctively knew he had pneumonia. On more than one occasion, I took him to the hospital and told them, "The baby has pneumonia." Each time, the doctors would examine him and confirm my diagnosis.

There were other times where his motions were odd and sporadic. I suspected they were seizures, but they looked different from typical seizures. Another trip to the hospital identified a seizing problem, and the baby was put on anti-seizure medication.

The dilemma continued with him not eating sufficiently or gaining enough weight, so I requested a feeding tube for him. It's called a G-tube.

With the tube inserted directly into his stomach and tied off, he could then receive nothing by mouth. He would be machine fed only. But this caused another set of challenges.

I attached the feeding tube to the machine, which was designed to slowly administer food into his stomach throughout the night. But after a short time, the baby's belly would fill with gases. He would then cry from the pain and pressure.

With the G-tube, not only could he not take anything by mouth, he also could not bring anything up. I would then have to repeatedly interrupt the feeding by disconnecting the feeding tube and inserting a ventilation tube for periodic burping.

Using the G-tube machine was a long, tedious procedure that simply didn't work as they said it would. The whole set-it-and-forget-it intention was flawed by an inability to burp the baby as needed.

For that, I was able to construct a different idea. I asked the doctors if I could incorporate the use of a syringe with the G-tube, instead of having the machine pump it in. I suspected the machine was causing the excessive stomach gasses, even though it was a slow and steady feeding process. It was all intake for the baby, and the gasses just built up too quickly.

With the doctor's go-ahead, I eliminated the machine and slowly injected the food into the tube, letting it run in naturally. Gravity did the work from there, allowing the food to seep in. It worked very well. It eliminated the excessive gasses, and it was a much better feeding experience for him and me both.

We had this particular baby for at least two years. When he was about eighteen months old, he had to have a tracheotomy to help with his breathing problems. Still, the slightest cold posed a huge threat to him.

Sometimes the tracheal tube would fill with phlegm and required immediate suctioning. This would have to be done every fifteen minutes to maintain a clear airway. If it was badly blocked, I would have to quickly replace the tube to keep him breathing.

That baby needed a lot of care. It was as heartbreaking as it was tiring that he should have these permanent ailments, which could have been prevented.

Eventually, after repeated trips to the hospital with him, the baby's surgical nurse talked me out of taking him back to our home. He required constant attention. Our younger daughter, Myia, was a big help in providing much of his care, but it became an overwhelming task. He needed attention 24/7.

The baby was placed in a children's home, and I saw him at the hospital once after that. I was there with another of our foster babies and saw him being brought in from an ambulance. I immediately identified myself and inquired about his condition.

"Is he really sick?" I asked.

Their response: "No, this is how we transport him."

I wish I had known that. They utilized an ambulance and two attendants, and I had always taken him to the hospital by myself. It was by the grace of God that he didn't seize or choke or encounter any number of other problems while I took him back and forth on my own.

Along with these and all the typical scrapes and scrums of childrearing, with the butterfly kisses and butterfly stitches, I really have become a competent nurse—without the costly campus time.

8

Names in a Whisper

by Janet Brooks

When it comes to their children, most mothers have distinct, acute, highly sensitive hearing capabilities. *Mommy ears.* This explains why she can be roused from sleep by the proverbial pin drop, the slightest stirring, or the softest whimper. We are super heroes of sound; we can hear everything.

It's one thing to hear the telephone ring while running a vacuum sweeper; it's another thing to hear a whisper. I know this by experience.

I was running the sweeper, and I heard it clearly. It didn't come from a baby, however. It wasn't the sound of a child. It wasn't a human, external voice at all. But I heard it.

Like many mothers or workers of any description, I multi-task, and I do some of my most productive thinking while busy with other things. Some of my thought processes involve reflective prayer, and the whisper I heard on this particular day was a result of that practice.

Things were pleasant. All was well. It really was a wonderful life, as Amy said. I had a lot to be thankful for, and I truly was thankful. I was also a bit puzzled.

I was a three-time mom to Brian, Candy and Myia. As I maneuvered the vacuum sweeper I reflected on motherhood. I thought about how, when we were expecting Brian, only a boy name had come to me—*Brian*. So, when he was born, that's who he was without a second thought.

I had never had an ultrasound; not with Brian, not with any of my pregnancies. As expectant parents, Rich and I never knew what we were having. We found out the old-fashioned way—in the delivery room.

We didn't care what gender the baby would be. I did, however, make a request to God regarding hair and eye color with our first child. I prayed that the baby would have black hair and blue eyes.

Concerning traditional birth colors, I didn't know if blue or pink would be the prominent color of the day. Like placing a penny in a gumball machine, you take what you get. You may have wished for pink, but blue is just as good.

Blue gumball. Brian.

I did not know I was having a boy. I did not realize I was having a Brian. But that was the only name I had heard in my heart and mind.

As for my request, he does have black hair and blue eyes. All of our other children would come with brown hair and brown eyes. (Later, they would often ask why I didn't pray for them to have blue eyes also. I do have a thing for blue eyes, but I guess I didn't want to be greedy. I wanted to save some for other parents who might wish for the same).

When Brian's name first came to me, I had no suspicion that it might have been God's voice or that it was His way of tipping me off as to what we were having. Nor did I realize that this naming method would become a pattern.

The same happened with Candy; the name just came to me out of nowhere like a whisper. I did manage to think-up another girl's name, which I don't recall. This time there was no boy names. Try as I might, none surfaced.

Brian was four at the time. Without offering him any choices or suggestions, I asked him one day: "What name do you like for a baby sister?"

Without hesitation, he said, "Candy!"

"You mean Candy like what you eat? C-A-N-D-Y?" I asked.

He said, "Yes."

With having been the first name that had come to me, I knew Candy was meant to be. And so it was.

Pink gumball. Candy.

With my third pregnancy came the name Myia. I loved that name from the first time I heard it. Why hadn't I thought of it before? Why did it come to me then, during that pregnancy?

Myia was the name of a German gal with whom I had become friends while Rich was serving in the Army. We were living in Heidelberg, Germany at the time, and I became close friends with Myia. Her husband, like Rich, occupied a military transportation position.

It was the name Myia I heard while carrying our third child. And it was three-month-old Myia who napped while I ran the vacuum sweeper that day.

As I vacuumed, I silently prayed: "God, it's a good thing you gave us a girl with Myia because I have no idea what we would have named a little boy."

That's when I heard it, that whisper, crystal clear, "Noah."

I chuckled, "It's a fine time to give me one now!"

Five years later, Noah was born.

Gumballs and eye color aside, it was significant that each of their names came to me before they were born. It was as if I already knew them, spiritually introduced, and somehow acquainted with who they would become. They were already a part of me, a part of us.

When I answered Linda's telephone call on that particular October morning, it was eight years after Noah was born and thirteen years since his name had come to me. That's when it happened again.

As Amy has said, Linda stated that she had a baby girl that was born without arms or legs. With this unusual set of circumstances, Linda asked if we could come to the hospital to see the baby, to help determine if we would foster her, rather than simply having her delivered to our house.

I was certain we would take her in, but I agreed to the conditions. Yes, Rich and I would go to the hospital to see her, as soon as he got home.

When I hung up the telephone I heard the whisper yet again.

"Her name is Amy."

That's when I knew she was ours; not just for fostering but for keeps. "Amy" was not the codename assigned by Children's Services. It was not her issued name; it was her intended name. It came to me like the names of our other babies, and I instinctively knew she *was* our baby, our fifth child.

She needed a home. She needed a family. Ours would be it.

Birthparents and lineage unknown. Limbs or not. None of that mattered. She already had my heart, and she already had a name.

Amy!

Introduction

Meet My DAD

Before Mom continues with more on my infancy, I'd like to introduce my dad and allow him to contribute to the drama. Be warned: he types even slower than Mom. You might want to make yourself a sandwich. Sit back, put your feet up if you have them, and make yourself comfortable; we could be here a while.

To secure Dad's input is a great achievement, given his anonymous and ambiguous disposition. If Mom is the "thump" of the family heartbeat, Dad is the silent pause in between. His demeanor is practically inaudible and nearly invisible.

Yet, this doesn't completely illustrate his personality. I know he does have one, somewhere, but it's hard to describe. He's sort of like a human Bobble Head.

He's like an artist's rendering, and very realistic looking.

That isn't to imply that he just sits around gathering dust. Far from it. He has always been a hard worker and a good provider.

Among other things, Dad is our resident thing-fixer. He's a true craftsman. He's a thinker, a tinkerer, an inventor of sorts. He's also a talented mechanic and skilled woodworker. Most important, my dad is a man of high morals and deep convictions. He's an awesome father.

Dad's a keeper, like a collector's item. I wouldn't trade him for anything in the world. He isn't for sale either. If he was, you couldn't afford him. No one could. Like the rest of my family, he is precious and priceless.

Dad has always been a strong arm to lean on, the go-to guy for problem solving. Listening is what he prefers over speaking. I can't imagine why this trucker would have a CB radio in his rig, if not merely for listening to it.

Mom has often told a joke that if Dad was ever in need of surgery and they cut open his belly, a long-suppressed laugh would inadvertently come roaring out of his innards.

He is one who favors quiet observation over noisy interjections. Never has he offered a kneejerk reaction or an offhanded remark.

My dad, Richard Brooks, is a man of knowledge and silent wisdom. Countless times, I have asked him countless questions, especially in my youth. After a while, he would ask, "Are you writing a book?"

I would always say, "Yes."

To that, he would reply, "Skip that chapter."

Now I really am writing a book, and I know he would prefer I skip this chapter. I also know the book would look funny with these pages being blank.

Thanks, Daddio, for filling them in.

2

Life on Wheels

by Richard Brooks

A my would tell you I'm an inventor. If I am, the wheel was not among my ideas. I didn't invent it, and I never sought to reinvent it. But I have used it, along with brute diesel power and perpetual motion, to take care of my family.

I suppose wheels are to me what babies are to Janet. Caring for kids and babies has always been her true gift and calling. While I have continually supported and assisted that, my rightful title is *"provider,"* and my profession has always been driving.

For me, driving far exceeded the standard type, and the machines I'd come to operate would greatly outweigh the one I first started in.

A black 1947 Pontiac Slant Back: that was my first car, my very own set of wheels. It was in good condition, and it ran well for the years and miles it had seen.

My first job was at a gas station, owned by Janet's uncle. The man had a brand-new 1953 Catalina, but he liked my car so much that he often borrowed it to run his errands. Driving my car was a treat for him. Driving anything was a treat for me. Soon I'd come to make a career of it.

After a couple of years at the gas station, I took a job with a lumber company making deliveries in 6-wheel trucks. That led me down the road of life-long trucking, a career that seemed to get interrupted a few years into it.

It happened only eleven months after Janet and I were married. That's when I was drafted into the Army.

After being processed at Fort Knox, Kentucky, I went for my eight weeks of basic training at Fort Benning, Georgia. From there I would do eight weeks of advanced training at Fort Leonard Wood, Missouri.

Janet was able to follow me to Leonard Wood, but she had to live off post. She visited me in the evenings, and I was free to stay with her on the weekends.

My designation at Leonard Wood was Heavy Equipment Operator, but I was trained in what I had already been doing—driving trucks. As it turned out, my career didn't suffer such an interruption, after all. It just took an alternate route, which is something drivers are accustomed to.

When I finished my training, I was deployed to Heidelberg, Germany, an E4 with the 519th transportation company: Head Quarters Special Troops USAREUR (United States Army Europe).

My duties involved driving one General Mitchell and others of his staff from point A to point B and back in the general purpose (GP) military vehicle commonly called the Jeep.

I was allowed to live off post in Heidelberg, and after I got settled there, I brought Janet over. That was where I did the last eighteen months of my two-year military invite, and that was where our son, Brian, was born. He's our firstborn and our only child with a dual citizenship.

As for driving, it's what I'd always do. It became a permanent part of my life. Eventually, I'd be living on wheels, while making a living on them.

I'd never be without having a set of wheels under me, which is better than me being under them, I suppose. The motion of forward rolling or backward parking was a constant. It was my skill, and it put food on our table.

Upon returning to civilian life, I accepted a union driving position, operating 10-wheelers. After driving for that company for fourteen years, I bought a tractor-trailer rig and went into business for myself as an owner-operator.

That venture took me zigzagging across the country, hauling the proud symbol of Pittsburgh—steel. Lots of it. But it took a while to get that operation up to speed, literally speaking.

Before owning my own rig, I had never even driven an 18-wheeler. On my first run, it took me all night to get from Pittsburgh to Hammond, Indiana. I was hauling what we called slinkies. They are large rolls of wire, and I was afraid the bindings would come loose. So, I drove cautiously and kept stopping to check them every so often.

I was always driving, always rolling, always associated with sets of wheels.

When I wasn't driving truck, I was driving Janet and the babies to and from hospitals or doctor visits. As foster parents, we were required to constantly attend meetings. More driving.

Like most dads, I also drove our kids around and kept up with their activities when I was home. My entire adult life has been about driving.

Me and wheels.

Janet and babies.

These were constants.

In 1995, I received the "Ryder's District Driver of the Year Award." Throughout my entire career, I've never hurt anyone, never fallen asleep at the wheel, never run off the road, never backed over a mailbox, never hit a squirrel. However, I did somehow manage to acquire a couple of speeding tickets—one in Pennsylvania and one in Ohio.

To this day, I'm not sure how those occurred, but I do know there's big money in ticketing big trucks, and there's often unwanted, individualized attention directed to those who drive them.

My truck was governed to only run no more than 60 MPH. So, with the hammer down, I could never drive it like I stole it, even if I wanted to. Yet, I was selected to make a generous donation to the Highway Patrolman's Association, not once but twice.

Sooner or later, it happens to everyone who drives a truck. It's like being fingered, randomly, as a perpetrator in a rolling lineup of big rig mug shots.

In addition to the speeding tickets, I also experienced a couple of close calls. On those occasions, there were others chosen to empty their pockets, whether they were actually exceeding the speed limit or not.

Once, I was trucking through Ohio, headed east with a buddy and several others truckers. We were all in a line and a cop motioned for my buddy to pull over. The rest of us were ignored. We continued on, and he stayed behind to fellowship with the patrolman.

On another occasion, I was leading a string of truckers past the cornfields of Nebraska when we were all motioned to pull over as an entire fleet. After a few moments, I was waved off while the rest of the guys had to stay. I went on my way, with no choice but to leave some good men behind. I didn't really mind it too much, though.

In contrast to what is considered to be a flawless driving record, I have been involved in two accidents over my lifetime. The first one was on the job, while driving the 10-wheelers.

It happened on a two-lane highway, at the bottom of a hill, near Uniontown, Pennsylvania. I was making a left-hand turn at an intersection when a dump truck came barreling down the hill behind me. I don't recall if the driver had brake failure or what, but he was passing everyone in his way, and he slammed into my left side as I made my turn.

The impact was enough that it forced my truck into a neighboring gas station, and I remember seeing my truck's battery skidding across the pavement. Yet, I received only a scratch on my head. Other than that, no one was hurt. With the nearby gas pumps, it could have been big.

The second accident was several years later, during my 18-wheeler years. It wasn't a trucking accident; it involved our family vehicle. That crash was more senseless and completely avoidable. It was one that would effectively end my career as an owner-operator.

Amy was part of that one, and she will write more about it later. She was five years old at the time. (No, she wasn't driving.) The summary of it for me is that I sustained a herniated disc, which put me out of work for more than a year. That was the first and only time in my adult life that I wasn't driving.

My recovery was slow and painful, and it was during that time that I sold my rig. I had no income, and by then, I had had my fill of long hauls and nights away from home. I was ready to do something else. As it turned out, that "something else" would be more driving.

When my previous employer of fourteen years heard that I was out of work, they called and ask if I'd like to return to my old job. I accepted and went back to driving their 10-wheelers. The company then graduated to 18-wheelers, and I returned to driving those on short runs, mostly to neighboring states. No more long hauls. No more being away from home at night.

Wheels—that's what much of my life was about.

Eventually, I retired from trucking, but I continued to work for that company for several years, filling orders on a part-time basis by moving the trucks in and loading them with a forklift.

More driving, more wheels.

I have recently retired completely, bearing the intent of sitting down without staring through a windshield or watching side view mirrors. And I am looking forward to reading Amy's book under these conditions.

This is present tense, however.

With that, I'd like to reference a time long before the injury accident, long before my long-haul days were ended. On that particular day, I had my rig for only two years.

I was tending to it—tending to my wheels—as usual and in a literal sense. It was part of a day's work. It came with owning a rig. I was at the local truck shop having new tires put on my tractor when I was told I had a phone call.

It was Janet.

She asked how long I would be with the truck. She said we'd have to go to the hospital when I got home. There was a baby girl we'd have to meet and bring home with us.

She then relayed to me what Linda had told her: "The baby doesn't have any arms or legs."

"Oh my goodness! What are we gonna do with her?" I asked.

"Don't worry," she said. "Things will work out, somehow."

I hung up the phone knowing she was right, considering the experiences we had had with the other babies. Still, when I turned my attention back to my truck and its wheels, I couldn't help but wonder what other turns and twists lay in the road ahead of us.

Such is the existence of a trucker, and such is the life of a foster parent. You just have to keep on rolling, no matter what or who comes along.

10

Early Tears

by Janet Brooks

When I saw Amy for the first time, I loved her, immediately. I can easily understand why Dr. Alexander did too, and I'll never understand why the couple who produced her did not. There was just something special about that particular baby.

Amy had a sweet, pleasant disposition and such warmth about her. At only eight days old, she was squeaky clean and wrapped in innocence. Rich and I took her home, bright-eyed, content, and oblivious to her abandonment.

Agreeing to accept her seemed so natural and right. It was all proper and businesslike. From there we followed our normal schedule, and everything was fine that first night.

After dinner that evening, we all attended our midweek church service—Amy included. At its conclusion, we gathered together and prayed God's blessings and guidance over Amy.

I specifically asked God that He would grant her to somehow be able to walk someday and that she would gain enough independence to be able to do things for herself.

With that I felt a spontaneous notion to include an additional request. Maybe it was bold faith or maybe I wanted a sign that God had heard our prayers and that His hand would be on her life. I placed my fingertip on the purple birthmark covering Amy's nose and mouth and added a plea that God would remove the birthmark from her face.

Back at home, it was a typical night with a newborn in the home. Amy slept like a baby, which means she was obedient to nature's clockwork and awoke every four hours. It was all very commonplace. Nothing out of the ordinary, nothing unique, nothing greatly notable.

The next morning was a different story, however. When it came time to bathe her, it struck me. In the act of dressing her, I slipped a tiny tee shirt over Amy's head and reached for arms to pull through. That's when the reality of it all set in. That's when it all became extremely real.

It hit me, and it hit me hard.

With this soul crushing realism came tremendous grief for this beautiful newborn. I then experienced what I call my waterloo. I ached for this dear, innocent baby, and I broke down like an old car on a barren stretch of highway. I cried for her until I could cry no more. It was a true watershed moment.

Eventually, the cloud passed and the burden lifted. I had experienced that one necessary cry and I was okay. I was all cried out, and all was well. Or so I thought.

Just a few days later, I was holding Amy, rocking her, feeding her a bottle. That's when it happened again. I looked toward the ceiling and cried.

Pouring out my heart and my tears to God, I prayed, "Why couldn't she have been born with arms? Or why not at least with just one arm?"

Adding to the unfairness was that this precious baby had become a quick distant memory to those who were supposed to love her most. In one fell swoop, they had written her off and forgotten her by the time their feet touched the pavement of the hospital parking lot.

With all this, my stomach wrenched with sobbing. My soul moaned. My heart mourned. My tears rolled.

After a while, I looked down and saw the most bewildered look on Amy's face. As she took her bottle, she looked up at me with her huge dark eyes.

She didn't stir. She didn't fuss. She didn't seem afraid, just puzzled. I then realized my tears had been dripping from my face onto hers.

Babies typically don't produce their own tears until they are a few months old. At this very early age, Amy had never experienced tears on her face until then. Mine were her first.

At that instant, something happened inside me. I wiped the tears from Amy's face and from mine. I gathered myself, and I decided there'd be no more crying over Amy's birth condition. It was what it was. So goes the idiomatic phrase: "It is what it is." As much as I would have liked, there was nothing that could be done to change it.

So, I entered into a covenant with God, right then and there in that rocking chair, in the living room of our home. I said, "God, I'm done crying. I'm not going to do it anymore. If You will show me how to raise her, I'll do everything the best I can."

I somehow knew, from that moment forward, things would truly work out. Of this I was quite certain.

11

Miracle Dismissed

by Janet Brooks

Explaining the unexplainable can be a difficult task, especially when attempting to submit spiritual rationale to a highly educated professional. I discovered this in the doctor's office when I took Amy for her first checkup.

It was essentially her one-month examination, but she was between six to eight weeks old by the time she could be worked into the schedule.

When that day arrived, the kids were in school, and Rich was working. It was just me and Amy, setting out for what would be her first of many medical road trips. Off we went.

What was expected to be a routine appointment didn't turn out to be so routine for the doctor.

Amy's health check was fine, but the doctor indicated there might have been a problem with her medical file. Quite bewildered, he studied the charts, and he looked at Amy.

From baby to charts, from charts to baby. As if watching a game of table tennis—back and forth—he examined the records, and he looked at Amy.

Finally, the doctor muttered his confusion. He stated that, according to the records, this baby was supposed to have a significant birthmark covering a substantial portion of her face.

By that time, she didn't.

It was gone!

"I don't understand," he said. "What happened?"

I could appreciate the man's turmoil, especially from a medical standpoint. After all, a port-wine stain is called a stain for a reason. They are nature's unwanted tattoos that have no resemblance of any real body art. They contain no intelligent pattern, and they consist of no rational form or attractive design. They are there for no explicable reason, and they serve no useful purpose. Most notable is the fact that they remain for a lifetime.

These stains cannot be bleached, blanched, whitened, or discolored. No amount of rubbing, scrubbing, buffing, or polishing could remove them. There's no secret formula. There's no prescription, cream, potion, or pill to eliminate them.

They cannot be eradicated. They'll never be erased. None have been redacted or extracted. There are no magical recipes or mystical concoctions. They simply don't go away.

Yet, Amy's had become nonexistent.

To my household it was a blessing, but we weren't as astonished by it as the doctor seemed to be. Years prior, we had experienced a medical miracle with Myia.

When she was thirteen months old, Myia developed a herniated naval. It happened while she was learning to walk, and we suspect it was due to abdominal exertion from when the older kids walked with her. They would hold her arms up to balance her as she walked, and we believe it generated excessive strain, causing the hernia.

These don't go away either. They don't heal on their own or disappear; they have to be surgically repaired.

At church we prayed for Myia, and within three days the protrusion and its discoloration had completely disappeared. She had no pain, no discomfort, and no bulge.

This time it was Amy. Her birthmark went off to wherever Myia's hernia did. It was just gone. We had asked God to remove it for her, and He saw fit to grant that petition. All that remained, and does to this day, is a tiny inconspicuous spot. It is a beauty mark on a beautiful face.

Though she chooses to conceal it with makeup, it serves as a small lingering reminder of Amy's first miracle. It is miniscule evidence of answered prayer.

When I tried to explain this to the doctor, he looked at me like I was crazy or as if I were a two-headed dragon that had just swooped down from an alternate universe. He quickly dismissed the notion of prayer and miracles. Apparently, it doesn't mix well with medical theology.

I had to simply smile and leave well enough alone, but the proof remains because the birthmark no longer does.

Doctors are wonderful. They are greatly respected and ever in demand, but sometimes God doesn't mind baffling them by doing the impossible. He's been known to throw an occasional wrench or two into their entire practice.

It's not that He would want to embarrass anyone, it simply strengthens our faith and offers us hope. For some, to embrace the invisible is preposterous. For me, to reject a visible miracle is more so. To this day, Amy's beautiful, unblemished face is a true reflection of this observation.

12

Baby Gifts

by Janet Brooks

Babies come in different sizes, shapes, weights, and colors. They arrive purely innocent, with a clean slate into a new, unexplored world. Some emerge healthy and whole. Others not so much. Some have certain advantages or privileges. Others have less.

Each is unique and individualized. As they grow and develop and step through life, there can be no substitute for any of them. They could never possibly be replaced by another. No one shares their fingerprints. Their DNA is matchless.

All are precious gifts, and many are gifted.

Teenagers are an entirely different story. They are a species unto themselves. I suggest all teenagers be shipped to a remote island and be brought back after they grow some brains, but babies are wonderful. There are no two alike. Yet paradoxically, they are all the same.

All babies know what they need and want, and crying is their natural impulse and their universal means of communicating those needs. They know when they are hungry. They know when they are in any type of discomfort. They know when they want to be held and nurtured.

Babies understand the moods and emotions around them, such as anger or adoration. They all come with the same fears—those of loud sounds and the sensation of falling. They sense danger. They respond to vocal tones and facial expressions. They understand resentment and rejection as equally as love and acceptance.

A baby doesn't have to be taught how to suckle; it comes naturally to them for comfort as much as for nourishment. Some begin to instinctively suck their thumb immediately after birth. They all breathe, sleep, and perform other necessary bodily functions without prompt or instruction.

At five to six months, they begin to roll over; typically from back to belly, and then from belly to back. Usually they are strong enough to begin sitting up at that age. At six to seven months, they begin to crawl. At about a year, they begin to walk, and the world is theirs for the taking.

Now, enter a baby born with Tetraphocomelia. You'd expect the rules to change. You'd anticipate great exceptions. There should be prominent limitations, if not complete and utter helplessness.

With Amy this wasn't the case.

Believe it or not, she was on target with most of her basic developments. She did get off to a different start from other babies. Different is what her whole life would be about. It came as a matching set—altered birth condition, altered lifestyle—but she was never deterred.

She was never completely handicapped.

As her foster parents, we were subject to the rules and requests of CYF. Among their ideas was to have Amy undergo some facets of physical therapy, so she could learn the fundamentals of infantile development. With this, we were required to take her to the hospital for a therapist to work with her to roll over. It wasn't successful, and we stopped taking her after a few sessions.

It could have been that they were intimidated by working with a limbless baby, but some of their ideas and attempts were not only ineffective, they were quite ridiculous.

Back at home, it was Rich who observed what was preventing Amy from successfully rolling over. Rich was watching her one day as she tried to roll over on the floor, and he said, "I see what the problem is. She needs to lift her head a little."

Rich lifted Amy's head as she attempted to roll, and she flipped right over. With that discovery and achievement, he kept working with her.

He rolled her back over and lifted her head, and she flipped onto her belly again. After only a few times, she learned that she could roll over by lifting her head. And that was that. This "football baby" soon represented a good fumble; she just rolled all over the place.

If she could fit there, she would roll there, but her favorite spot was beneath the potted palm tree I had growing in the living room. It was a few feet tall. Amy would often roll over to it and just lay there on her back, staring up at it for the longest time. I have no idea what was going through her little mind, but she loved that palm tree.

As for sitting up, I had to work with her a little extra, to help strengthen her abdominals and lower back, but it wasn't really anything out of the ordinary. By using her little arms and by employing more wiggling motion than most babies, she also learned to crawl—infantry style.

Unlike other babies, Amy couldn't instinctively grab for toys and play with them. Rich used some creativity to counter this. He split a little plastic football in half, lengthwise, creating a makeshift prosthetics socket. He then placed the halves on the ends of her arms and secured them with non-allergenic tape. After that, he taped drinking straws to the little footballs.

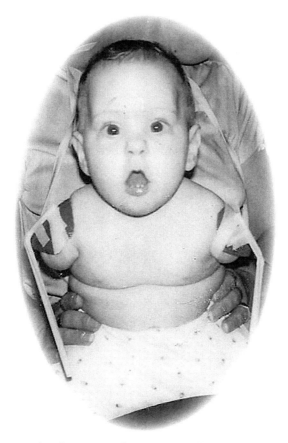

Straws...drinking utensils or arms...what's the difference?

The tape didn't stay on for very long before working loose, but it held long enough to allow Amy to sit and bat at her toys. Weebles were her favorite. We would put her in her highchair, which had an oversized tray, and she'd have a world of fun batting those toys around on it.

At eight months, Amy essentially broke herself of the bottle. It happened one day when Rich was drinking Pepsi from a disposable cup with a lid and a straw. He was holding Amy on his lap, and she leaned over and placed her mouth on the end of the straw.

I picked up the drink and capped the straw by placing my finger over the end of it, creating a vacuum and trapping the liquid inside. I then allowed Amy to sample the pop, as I released it into her mouth from the straw.

When I returned the straw to the cup, she again placed her mouth on it, and she instinctively began sucking the Pepsi through the straw. Never had any of our babies done that.

Whether ours or a foster baby, none had ever drank through a straw anywhere near that age. What's more, from then on, she was hooked. Amy would no longer take a bottle; the only way she would drink her milk was through a pop straw in a cup.

Completely and instantly weaned from a bottle and drinking through a straw at eight months? That was unheard of. While it may not have qualified her as a baby genius, it did cause us to think that this little girl was going to grow to be someone gifted and special. We were right about that.

13

Accessories Not Included

by Janet Brooks

A ccepting Amy was "winner-take-all" with what she had and didn't have. At the start, we weren't exactly sure of what we had signed up for, but we were signed up. We were committed to Amy, and we were in it for keeps.

Her rejection at birth was our gain for life.

Amy's birth condition became the source of a lot of added fuss and attention. However, much of that affection was different from the typical swooning over a new baby; it was sympathetic. Many regarded her as someone to be pitied.

When one particular woman at church saw Amy for the first time, she started going on about this poor, unfortunate baby not having any arms or legs. I immediately countered her sympathy with humor.

I told the woman we had purchased Amy from the Sears catalog. "You know how it is when you order something from those catalogs," I said. "It always arrives being the wrong color or the wrong size, or there are parts and pieces missing."

Concerning the things that were missing, Rich and I believed Amy would eventually require some sort of real prosthetics to help her to function in a normal manner. Arms constructed of drinking straws wouldn't cut it for long, but we had no idea as to when or how things would progress for her.

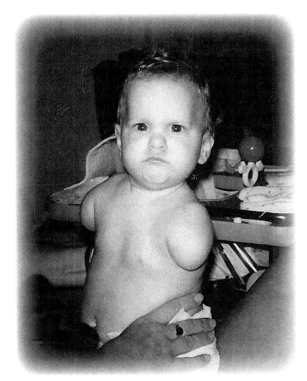

Whatchu talkin' 'bout, Willis?

The Sears catalog didn't carry the parts she'd need, and there was no local Limbs-R-Us in the immediate area, so Amy's journey into the world of prosthetics began at Pittsburgh Children's Hospital at less than a year old.

Using more durable material, the staff there attempted to replicate the straw arms that Rich had made, but they couldn't. After a short time, the doctors grew frustrated. Amy did too. As if she could read their guesses or sense their inabilities, she wanted no part of their efforts. The project was soon abandoned without any prosthetics for her.

Unintentionally and unaware, Amy seemed to become a bit of a celebrity to those who had contact with her and to those who had merely heard about her. Certainly she was unique, but it was as if she had become the world's newest and tiniest rock star. Before long, many goodhearted, caring people stepped forward to help make her life better.

With this, a variety of inventions came and went over a period of time. Some were more practical and helpful than others. Amy will cover more of those things later, picking up on what she remembers of them.

At a little more than a year old, Amy learned to feed herself with a spoon attachment. The utensil was fastened to a thick band that slid over her right arm. It was something that was being used successfully by others with damaged or deformed hands.

Eating with spoon attachment for the very first time

Ironically, the invention was recommended by Dr. Alexander at the D.T. Watson Institute, in nearby Sewickley, Pennsylvania.

This is the same Dr. Alexander who had been the head of the Cerebral Palsy department at Children's Hospital, the same Dr. Alexander who would have taken the newborn Amy home with him if he could have.

He was now with D.T. Watson, causing his and Amy's paths to cross again, and he thought the gadget might work well for Amy. It did.

The spoon attachment greatly assisted Amy's eating capability. To her it was a hand. With it she even quickly mastered the art of eating spaghetti, with minimal damage to the kitchen and neighboring properties.

Drinking from a cup for the very first time
(I've never had a drinking problem)

Basghetti...YUM!

Amy used the spoon attachment for a few years. When she got older, she also fed other babies with it, including her nephew, Wade. Without the attachment, Amy also became skilled at eating corn on the cob. She simply squeezed the ears of corn between the endpoints of her little arms and munched away.

At around the same time that she began using the spoon attachment, an organization offered to provide Amy with prosthetic arms, the design and construction of which was their own. Their hearts were in the right place. Their intention was good, but their work wasn't. They were not prosthetists, and their effort proved it.

The limbs were made of hard plastic, and they were much too heavy. Plus, they were designed for an older, larger child, and they were never modified for someone Amy's size.

Maybe they figured she would adjust and grow into them. Consequently, they were abnormally long. They looked like monkey arms, and they didn't work at all. Rich and I did appreciate the effort, though, and it gave us hope that useful prosthetics could eventually be made for Amy.

To our delight, we learned that Union Artificial Limb & Brace, in Pittsburgh, had been working on a single arm design for her. It was the right arm only, as to not overwhelm Amy with multiple prosthetic limbs.

Amy took possession of the arm at about fourteen or fifteen months of age. She was fitted with it at D.T. Watson after it was personally delivered there by Union's owner.

Rich and I called the limb a banana arm. It was a suitable moniker following the monkey arms, and we referred to it as such because of its look. The arm was shaped like a banana, mimicking the natural bend of a semi-relaxed human arm. Amy was able to successfully use that prosthesis for about three years or so.

The arm was secured to Amy with straps. For a hand there was a claw-like hook made of durable rubber composites.

When Dr. Alexander and his staff initially strapped the arm on Amy, they showed her how she could open the hook by drawing her shoulder inward and close the hook by pushing her shoulder outward.

She adapted to it immediately. There were no further instructions, follow-ups, or physical therapy needed. It was like a natural arm to her.

Amy didn't wear the arm at all times, but when she did, she used it very effectively—mainly for intricate things and for grasping items that were out of reach.

Banana Arm

With or without prosthetics, Amy didn't really know much different. She was a typical growing child—bright-eyed, inquisitive, and rambunctious. She was full of life, and she wanted to live it like everyone else.

With Amy, to get a large, family-size portion of joy and excitement, all we had to do was add water. A small segment of her early-life rehabilitation experience came with an introduction to aquatic therapy at D.T Watson. She loved it. Swimming came naturally for Amy, and she did well at it.

Anyone looking for a heaping dose of inspiration can find it in watching a limbless toddler swim in water that is much deeper than she is tall.

As for the Brooks kids, Amy was just another baby in the house, another kid to play with. They didn't treat her differently or act as though she was something special. To them she was not fragile or handicapped, which is probably why Myia saw fit to use her for a football.

To get a piggyback ride from Rich, Amy wasn't able to hold on in an upright position, like the other kids. So, Rich would get down on all fours and give her a ride like that. It was more a horsey ride, I suppose, but the representation of a barnyard animal, nonetheless.

Giddy-up, Daddio! Let's go pick up Mom and the other kids!

Lucky for Rich, this would not become Amy's continuing mode of transportation. In fact, to be sure of it, he designed a walker for her. He then submitted the concept to D.T Watson who subsequently built it.

This was roughly two or three months after Amy got the banana arm. The walker was constructed of chrome-plated tubing with four casters. To hold Amy upright, the framework contained two padded torso supports. Everything was adjustable and locked into position with thumbscrews. It was a great invention, and Amy scooted all over in that thing.

'Cause that's how I roll!

Of course her first stop was the potted palm tree. It was like a magnet that pulled her straight to it. We put her in the walker not knowing how she would react, being her first test drive.

It was a good thing Rich didn't bother to mount a rearview mirror on the walker because Amy wouldn't have checked it. Even better was that there was no other living room traffic; she wouldn't have yielded the right of way.

As soon as Amy was placed in the walker, she made a beeline for the palm tree. When she reached it, her first point of business was to conduct a soil sample.

She just plopped her face into the potting soil at the base of the palm tree, and she quickly came up spitting dirt. From that moment on, she didn't have quite the same level of fascination with the palm tree. She did love that walker though.

A 16-year-old in a flashy new sports car couldn't have recorded more miles than Amy did in the year-and-a-half that she used the walker.

She would scoot off somewhere and say, "Could you bring me my arm, please?"

Someone would take Amy the banana arm, and she would sit and play—dressing her dolls like any other little girl would do. When she was done playing, she would sling the arm off and scurry to her next destination.

At nearly three years of age, Amy went from the walker to duck feet. That's exactly what they looked like. This invention was a one-piece unit consisting of a molded plastic torso socket, two metal legs, and a pair of orange wooden flat-bottom feet—duck feet—also manufactured by Union.

If it walks like a duck and quacks like a duck...it's not...it's just Amy!

The legs of this specific invention were rigid; they had no give or shock absorption. To move the feet, Amy would use a waddling motion, shifting her weight from side to side. The duck feet worked, but they were clumsy and clunky.

Rich inspected them and quickly devised an alteration to improve them for Amy. "They need springs," he said.

Rich's terse, three-word suggestion led to a quick modification with a spring inserted into each of the lower legs. It was a great improvement, but with the upgrade came heightened concerns.

Amy was scary on those duck feet. We did our best to teach her that, if she fell, she'd have to turn her head to protect her face.

One particular doctor was not in favor of Amy having prosthetic legs of any design. Kids fall enough as it is, and the idea of a no-armed toddler trudging around on stilts didn't set well with him.

While I was concerned with Amy sustaining a facial injury, this doctor was thinking far beyond chipped teeth or a fractured nose. He was afraid that, if Amy fell and did irreparable damage to her shoulders, her entire future and quality of life would be in extreme jeopardy.

Thankfully, that never happened.

As it turned out, she didn't stay in the legs for more than a few months. One day she was sitting on Rich's lap, and she said, "I wanna walk."

Rich placed her on the floor. "Okay," he said. "I'll get your legs."

Amy said, "No. Me do. I walk."

Off she went, toddling across the floor on only her hips. That was the end of the duck feet and the end of Amy walking on manufactured legs. To her, those particular add-ons became instantly unnecessary. They were just extra luggage and added weight, apparently.

She was right; she could do.

I had prayed that Amy would be able to walk someday. That prayer has been answered; she did walk, and she does walk, excluding the duck feet or other unnecessary accessories.

14

Part of the Family

by Janet Brooks

Obtaining functional prosthetic limbs for Amy was generally a side issue, though we greatly desired for her to have them. Of more immediate importance to us was obtaining Amy, permanently. To adopt her was nothing quick or easy, if it would even be at all possible.

Back then, it was especially difficult for foster parents to actually adopt a child they were fostering. The system wasn't set up for that. We had no long-lasting custody rights, and we had no say about where or when a child would be adopted, or by whom.

We were not adoptive parents. Our duty was to provide temporary care for babies who would either return home to their birth parents or be adopted by other would-be parents who were waiting. Our role was fostering, plain and simple.

In addition to this, Rich and I were outside the norm of typical adoptive parents. Many younger, childless couples eagerly awaited parenthood through natural or adoptive measures. We were blessed with four healthy, growing children of our own. This likely could work against us.

However, it was as much a matter of perspective as it was a matter of policy. In contrast, we were viable candidates because we had proven our abilities as natural parents and as capable foster parents. Simply put, we had a good track record.

We had cared for Amy since she was eight days old, and we had all bonded with her—and she with us. Ours was the only family she knew. Amy wasn't a nameless object, and to us she wasn't a limbless baby; she was *our* baby. Amy was completely adjusted, well cared for, and deeply loved by us all.

The reasoning could work both ways, but the guidelines were not in our favor. Policies are policies, rules are rules, and people who enforce them often do it well. In theory and in reality, Amy could have gone to someone else. Fact is, that was the intended goal of the CYF.

I was informed early on by Doreen that we couldn't keep Amy; we couldn't officially adopt her. "Janet, I have to put her out there," she stated. "I have to make her available for outside adoption."

In response, I insisted, "We will have an attorney, and we will adopt her."

Rich and I started the paperwork and initiated the adoption proceedings when Amy was about six months old. We knew we had a long road ahead of us. It was good that Rich was a trucker; he was well acquainted with long roads and accustomed to riding out enduring times.

We would persist and ride it out together. What's more, we would do it as a family unit because the Brooks kids were as much in favor of adopting Amy as Rich and I.

To the kids, Amy was already like a sister, and everyone was highly in favor of making her an official part of the family; so much so that we held a family conference to decide on a middle name for her.

Everyone weighed in. One recommended Amy Lu, another offered Amy Jo. Back and forth we went until I suggested Amy Beth.

The name seemed to resonate. It carried a waft of sophistication mixed with a gust of significance. Much like when the name Amy had come to me in a whisper, it just hung in the air, and it felt right.

It was unanimous; if she were to become ours, she would be Amy Beth. But things with the adoption were not progressing nearly as smoothly or as rapidly as we would have liked. For the couple who produced Amy, it was quick and easy to give her away. For us, our fight to keep her was much more difficult and time-consuming.

Adding to the theatrics and uncertainty was an unknown woman who expressed an interest in taking Amy, and she did so in a very belligerent manner.

Maybe it was due, in part, to the woman's lack of professionalism and her abundance of rude aggression, which was boldly displayed in a vigorous letter writing campaign. Or maybe it was because Rich and I had adoption proceedings in motion by that time. Whatever the single cause or string of reasons, the CYF declined the woman's appeal and told her the baby was already being adopted.

We knew at that point we had rounded the corner, and we were excited about Amy becoming ours, legally and completely. The process was nothing simple, but we knew it would all be worth it because Amy was worth it.

There was the never-ending pile of paperwork, the attorney fees, and the countless meticulous details. Literally, every "i" had to be dotted and every "t" crossed. This fact increased the drama right up to the very end.

After more than a year-and-a half's investment, Rich and I appeared before the judge. We were ready to finish things up, and we were geared to make it happen. We were confident that we were completely prepared and that everything was in order. All the criteria had been met.

The papers were weighted with black ink; each blank was filled in and properly signed. Everything was organized, authorized, and notarized. We were stapled and stamped, validated and insigniated. (If you'll excuse some hillwilliam terminology.)

What a pleasant day it was! There we sat before the judge, Rich and I and all the kids—Brian, Candy, Myia, Noah, and Amy. We were proud as peacocks, and we had all our ducks in a row. Never mind the differing bird euphemisms; the point being we were prepared.

Game on! Let's get 'er done!

After a long period of silence and substantial waiting, the judge cleared his throat, peered at us over the rim of his reading glasses, and told us—quite matter-of-factly—that we were minus one document.

"I will go ahead and grant this adoption under one condition," he announced. "I must have that paper in my hand within one hour or the entire adoption proceeding is null and void."

All of a sudden, we didn't feel so much like peacocks, and we would have gladly traded one of those metaphorical ducks for that missing piece of paperwork. The hourglass had been tipped, and the sand was trickling.

As luck would have it, the office of the attorney who had been handling our case was located catty-corner to the courthouse. We quickly made a mad dash to get over there, so we could graciously barge through the doors and claim the missing document.

It was all stressfully dramatic up to the last minute, but God favored us that day. There were still a few grains of sand yet to fall. In a real Indiana Jones moment, we slid beneath the wire in the final seconds.

Amy officially became Amy Beth Brooks on November 17, exactly 772 days after Rich and I first set our eyes on her. With all the apprehension and worry and dramatic affects, we would happily go back and do it all over again if necessary.

Sometimes I shudder to think that she could have gone to the woman who sent the nasty letters to the CYF. I hate to think of what Amy's life might have been like if we had lost her to them or to anyone. In an ironic, unimaginable twist, we were given a glimpse of how things might have turned out for Amy had things fallen differently.

It happened a few years later, long after Amy was officially adopted. A family friend of ours was visiting a relative in a nearby town. As she was leaving, her relative requested that our friend deliver a puppy to a particular address. The home was of an adoptive family who would customarily present a puppy to each of their newly adopted children.

The address was on our friend's route of travel, so she agreed to deliver the puppy. When she went to the home, she was startled by what she saw. The conditions were less than sanitary, and there was an abundance of special needs children in the home. Some appeared to be mentally challenged. Some were in wheelchairs. None appeared well cared for.

Our friend casually made reference to the children, and the woman said something shocking: "We were trying to get a baby girl who was born without arms and legs. Someone else got her instead, but we just know we were supposed to have her."

Our friend stood there speechless for a few seconds, realizing that she was speaking of Amy. Finally, she told the woman, "I know the family who got her, and she's in a good home. She's with a good family."

It's unsettling to think Amy could have ended up there. In reality, I find it chilling to consider that she could have ended up anywhere. As is the case with each of our natural born children, I would hate to imagine our life without Amy.

Call it what you want—motherly protection or human selfishness. Either way, I would never give her up for anything. Our lives, our home, our family would not be what it is without Amy. Truly, she has been kissed by God.

Not only has her birthmark been miraculously removed, she was also healed at a later time, which prevented her from having a *mandatory* operation, a *required* maintenance surgery on her right arm.

As Amy grew, these surgeries were needed in about three-year intervals because the stunted humerus bone grew to a sharp point and caused painful swelling at the endpoint of her arm. There was also cracking, bleeding, and oozing at that location.

As a cure, the surgeons had to go in and scrape the bone, rounding it off. Her left arm never grew to a point; it was always blunt and knob-like on the end, which is probably why the left arm is shorter than the right.

When she was three years old, Amy had her first of these surgeries. She had a second one three years later. When she was about nine, it appeared a third operation would be necessary for the same reason, just as the doctors had predicted.

Again, the endpoint of her arm began to swell and hurt and crack open. We were in church for an evening service, and Amy was in a lot of discomfort from this condition. I asked her if she would like to be prayed for, and she said yes.

Our pastor, Jeff Leake, prayed for Amy. She began to feel better right away, and the telltale symptoms improved. Before long, I was on the phone with the surgeon, explaining what had taken place.

It was a completely different and more pleasant conversation than the one that I had had with the other doctor who couldn't understand why Amy's port-wine stain had disappeared.

As a man of faith, the surgeon understood the positive effect of prayer and the miraculous results that so often occur from it. He essentially placed himself on standby. Hopefully, he isn't still standing because Amy never needed any further service from him.

Her arm has been fine ever since Pastor Jeff's prayer. The humerus bone has never bothered her after that, and it is pointed just enough to give her good use of it.

She can type and email and do a myriad of other things like no one would believe, not to mention her artwork. Amy learned basic computer skills in school, but she taught herself the advanced software and updated technology. She's as good with digital art as with her conventional art, though there's nothing conventional about her methods and process.

Though she insists that she isn't, Amy is an inspiration, a positive influence, and a set example to many. Amy says Rich is an inventor, but she is also; she has had to create ways to carry out the daily demands of her life.

She has had to improvise a lot and modify the way she does things, and most of it has not been easy. Much of it has been tough on her, but she has managed to smile through it all, regardless.

Some people mistakenly believe that a blind person has the inborn ability to automatically adjust to their sightlessness or that they are naturally given a physical and intuitive countermeasure to cope. Erroneously, they think those with vision impairment can flawlessly hear, feel, or smell without effort.

In reality, there is no involuntary compensation given to those who were born with, or somehow develop, physical challenges. There are no free adjustments. These heightened senses have to be developed and honed by those individuals. This is true of all disabilities. Remember, with a birth defect, you *lose* something. There is a missing piece or a malfunctioning part. Nature doesn't systematically offset it with something better.

Amy is the same way. She didn't come with training wheels or a roadside emergency kit. At birth she was wrapped in a regular hospital blanket, not the cape of a super hero. She has had to find ways to manage, mostly on her own.

Her attitude and her tenacity have been remarkable. Never has she given up on a task, and she has never been one to complain. Instead of wasting time grumbling or pouting, she wisely invests her energy by figuring out a solution.

Amy often has to use her mouth for certain things, but she has never *overused* it; she has never sassed us, spoken disrespectfully, or used bad language. Nor has she ever acted out or drawn attention to herself.

Amy is a blessing to us all. She radiates with light, she is filled with love, and she retains a true compassion for others.

Countless individuals, who face fewer challenges than Amy, walk through life with a chip on their shoulder. They hate and cause harm to others, often for no reason. And they regularly project an image of self-entitlement. Society owes them, apparently, because life has not been fair or the world has not been kind to them.

Amy has never complained. She has never asked, *Why this? Why me?* She simply lives her life, loving God and loving others.

When she grew old enough to realize that people were staring at her, I encouraged her to just smile and say hello. She did that, and she still does.

Amy is a living example of persistence. If we were unable to help her figure something out, she did it on her own. Whether putting on her makeup, using a sewing machine, or crafting complex art projects, Amy invents methods to accomplish the most difficult tasks.

Most would have never predicted that she'd do the things she's done. Shortly after her birth, one doctor was so gloomy and negative about Amy's future that he said she'd never do anything, that she'd just spend her whole life strapped in a chair. Obviously, Amy didn't hear that prognosis.

This doctor apparently shared the same hopelessness as the grandfather who suggested that Amy be put in a room and left to starve to death.

If this doctor had recommended a life of inactivity, Amy didn't follow his orders. If he was prescribing a dose of self-pity, she didn't take a single tablet. She just became busy growing and learning and trying to figure out what life was all about—just as any child does.

Amy has done so much by raw instinct and self-motivation that she had even taught and inspired those in the health care profession who had tended to her. It was Dr. Alexander who best confirmed this when he said, "Amy taught us everything we know."

As early as age five, Amy was also helping and teaching other children who had arrived with disabilities. One was a girl of about three years old; the other was a boy who was around seven months. Both were born with Tetraphocomelia.

The girl had no arms or legs. The boy had a slight portion of leg development and a little more arm growth than Amy—about to the elbow.

No one knew how to help them, and the parents were lost for answers. Considering the advancements Amy had made, the experts concluded that she might be more of an expert than they were. So, they had us bring her in to work with those kids.

Amy not only offered verbal and visible encouragement, she also demonstrated the techniques that she had developed to accomplish specific tasks. She taught the boy and girl how to use their mouths for certain things and how to improvise universally. Where the doctors, therapists, and parents were unable to effectively help these children, Amy did.

Amy has never sought the path of least resistance. Never taken the easy road. Never slacked with her household chores or school work. In fact, she graduated high school as an Honor's student. And school was no pleasure trip or social club for Amy.

One thing that was disturbing to me during Amy's school years was that there were times when her teachers didn't collect the homework that they had assigned to the class. Seeing Amy do all that work and invest all that effort and have it go unrewarded was something I didn't appreciate.

Many times, I wanted to call the school and lodge a complaint about it, but Amy forbade me.

Her character is amazing. Amy is eternally a Brooks. She has a place at the table and a spot in the family photo. And she holds a piece of our hearts forever.

15

Part of Me

by Amy

Those are my parents. Didn't I tell you Mom was the talkative one? Normally, she comes in a kid's size large. Yet, her chapters seem to reflect more of her professional, motherly side, her down-to-business, roll-up-your-sleeves-and-get-'er-done persona. She often uses that as her cover for being such an all-time goofball.

As for Dad, if he had actually spoken those 1,800 words of his chapter, we wouldn't hear another peep out of him for the next year or so.

We've all heard it said that kids don't come with operating instructions or with owner's manuals. They say parents don't have a handbook to follow.

I'm not fully convinced.

Being vertically challenged, I'm not aware of all the books on our shelves. There has got to be at least a quick reference guide somewhere up there because, as parents and as grandparents, Mom and Dad know what they are doing. They always have.

That or they are good at faking it. Either way, by guess or by golly, they seem to do things right, consistently—even when no one's looking.

Without them, who knows where I'd be? But let's not forget that I also have two brothers and two sisters who are equally incredible. Each of them is special in their own way.

They are all credited with my acceptance into the family.

Collectively, they may have all prevented me from going under the auction hammer or being placed on the shelf of the nearest thrift shop. Or I could have been marked half-off at the dollar store. Because of them, none of those situations ever presented themselves.

After Mom and Dad, the Brooks family all-star lineup begins with Brian. As you know, he's the oldest, the firstborn, the one with the custom ordered hair and eye color. Brian holds the dual citizenship, and he owns an extra layer of muscles to go along with it.

Brian is a lot like Dad, being the strong, silent type. Somehow, he has that innate ability to just shrug his shoulders and let everything roll off, unfazed.

Always calm, always cool, never gets his undies in a twist. That's Brian, and those are some of the qualities I admire in him. My spring is wound a lot tighter than his. I tend to worry about everything, and he doesn't worry about anything. He's just unfair like that.

Brian likes to work out a lot, and he has the bulk and strength to show for it. Though I once had monkey arms, he has always had gorilla arms. When necessary, Brian used to pick me up and carry me places. This served us both quite well; for him it was exercise, for me it was cheap conveyance. Free actually.

One time he took Mom and me to watch Noah play in a basketball game. Instead of having me sit at floor level in my wheelchair, Brian carried me all the way to the top row of the bleachers, allowing me to see the game from a different perspective.

Unfortunately, Noah was knocked into by an opposing player and had to exit the game early with a knee sprain. Even so, it was great of Brian to have toted me up there.

Today, he and his wife, Jodi, have kids of their own to haul around: Chas, Chase, Brandon, and Brianna.

Candy is the most sensitive and sentimental. She can cry over anything, but she's dependable, someone I can go to when the chips are down. She offers great emotional support when something's bothering me. Maybe it's because—unlike Brian—she's been bothered by things before.

Candy is patient and understanding. She can empathize, she can relate. And though she may not have Brian's muscles, Candy has picked me up, many times, with an encouraging word or a helpful anecdote.

She's very caring, and she has always been good at sharing some of her own life experiences to show how things work out okay in the end. But don't let her description or her name fool you. She isn't all sprinkled with sugar and jeweled in gumdrops; Candy is actually a tough cookie.

She and her husband, Andy, have added Wade and Samantha to the family.

Myia is the younger of my two sisters, and we have always had a special closeness. Our personalities are a lot alike, and our tastes are very similar. She has a pretty good eye for picking out things that I might like.

Myia and I have always hung out and done things together, including sunbathing, which is something she has loved to do from as far back as I can remember.

Baking ourselves beneath the summer sun is one of the many things we shared when I was little. While Brian has the darkest hair, Myia has the darkest skin because she remains a sunray junkie to this day. The woman is a human solar panel. Just plug her in, and Myia can light up a room of any size.

Myia is the one who introduced me to arts and crafts. We used to sit at the kitchen table together, painting Christmas ornaments and those little plaster houses that light up. I think they had miniature lighting inside, but considering Myia's ultraviolet radiation levels...

I remember Myia liked to use a ton of glitter, and I liked to mix paint colors. Even with unlimited choices, I always wanted to create my own.

After growing up and moving out, Myia has always lived nearby, and we have continued to do things together. She and her husband, Mike, currently live next door.

Their boys are Cameron and Bryce.

Noah is the last and youngest of the natural born Brooks' kids, but I'd hesitate to call him the baby of the family. First off, I know what it's like to be referred to as a baby when you're not one, and it isn't exactly flattering. Also, he's the tallest. Hence, the aforementioned basketball participation.

By the way, his knee is better now. Thanks for caring.

What's more, Noah was always the troublemaker of the family, mostly at school. Nothing bad or serious. He never veered to the wrong side of the tracks, so to speak. He was just an irritant, a nails-on-the-chalkboard type of nuisance.

I think that was due to boredom. School was too easy for both Noah and Brian. They were always the most intelligent of us kids, but it was never reflected in their grades because they didn't apply themselves to their class work.

Noah, in particular, seemed to do what he could to avoid his studies. This led him to the practice of annoyance, which he seemed to score very well in.

Yet, Noah has always had a good heart. While he might have gotten into trouble at school, not all of his time there was wasted. Not everything he did was mischievous. Noah always looked out for me, especially if he saw someone making fun of me.

I don't recall anyone ever being openly rude to me, but things were often said behind my back. If Noah got wind of it, he confronted the issue and put an end to it—in a nonviolent way.

Noah is no longer a troublemaker, but he still looks out for me. He's the one who takes me places when Dad isn't feeling up to it.

Noah's wife is Theresa. Their kids, Benjamin and Grace, complete my fine collection of nieces and nephews.

This is my family. They are unknown, unsung, unseen heroes. Together they sculpted a pleasant world and carved out a peaceful existence for me. As a single unit, they provided a clear and lighted path. They gave me a yellow brick road to follow. I have traveled it carefully and continue to do so.

If I ever reach the end of it, I might summons the courage to ask the Wizard for a brain. But what matters most is that I have a heart, and I know I do because it's thankful.

My brothers and sisters do not view me as an adopted sibling. Though I'm technically half a sister, I've never been their half-sister. To them, I'm not an off brand, a cheap sisterly knockoff, or aftermarket imitation.

I am not the black sheep of the family, and although I have red hair (when I take the time to color it as such), I've never been a redheaded stepchild. Nor do I hold a 2nd Class designation like Clarence Oddbody.

I am fortunate to be an equal part of such a crazy, goofy, loving family and to have them an equal part of me.

It takes a village to raise a village idiot, and I could not have possibly asked for any better villagers than them!

Introduction

Meet the Villagers

Apparently, everyone who owns a computer is a writer these days. If so, there are four additional names that can now be legally added to that elite group.

But their motive remains questionable.

They may claim to be transcending the concept of mandatory sibling reinforcement or extending beyond the jurisdiction of family support—or something to that affect.

Their guise might be that they are exceeding the limits of standard encouragement and basic reassurance.

Who knows?

Simply stated, my siblings have elected to cut in on my writing gig.

In some closed-door meeting or back alley agreement, they have each chosen to chip in a page or two—presumably with my best interest at heart.

Instead of cheering me on from the sidelines or merely offering some verbal backing, they have readily presented a physical contribution—seemingly for my benefit.

Was it a unanimous decision of love and adoration or an irrefutable conspiracy to become inherently famous?

Either way, they entered at their own risk.

That's just the kind of people they are. It's how they roll.

None of them consulted a professional or employed the use of a ghostwriter. It was just them and their keyboards, their doors closed, and their backs to the world.

Nobody knew that it was even happening except for absolutely everyone in the entire family—but me.

There was no way that I could have seen it coming, as did no one in the literary world. There was also no way that it could have been prevented.

The question is "why?"

Perhaps they were completely mesmerized by the glitzy and glamorous notion of typing out words and seeing them appear within the pages of a printed book.

Maybe it's the allure of bright lights and the promise of celebrity. Or, it could be the attraction of abundant wealth beyond their wildest dreams.

Whatever their angle, the end result is the following few pages. Hopefully, someone will be kind enough to inform them that this writing thing isn't as lucrative as they might want to believe.

In fact, for them, it pays nothing.

I am in the process of seeking a volunteer to break it to them for me. If you choose to be that bearer of bad news, please be warned; these individuals have proven to be a bit unpredictable at times.

Luckily, for you, it is generally in a good way.

Villager-1: Brooks siblings

by Brian

I could give one answer in regards to Amy—SHE IS AMAZING, but I am not so sure that completely covers Amy. In the twenty-plus years she has been a part of our family, my thoughts have changed from worrying about the things that she might not be able to do, to what will she accomplish next?

From the beginning, Amy has pretty much accomplished everything she ever attempted. If a person didn't know Amy and only saw her handwriting, received a text or email, they would never know or believe something about her was different. If you actually see her use her computer or phone, that's what is unbelievable. Amy has always accomplished her goals and has always wanted to do everything herself with minimal help. She finds ways to do anything she wants in her own unique way.

I think people would understand if she had a bad outlook on life, but I do not know a more upbeat and positive person than Amy. She loves to laugh and joke around even if the joke is on her...like when we have to remind her to take off her gloves and wipe her feet when she comes in from the snowy weather!

Amy is a HUGE hockey fan and also quite the football fan. I remember the time she texted me and said she needed my help. Amy told me she was getting into a Fantasy Football League and wanted me to help her pick her team players. She and I texted back and forth multiple times before the draft started at 7:00 pm.

After the draft started, Amy continued to text me asking about players that were available. Her texting was so fast and mine so slow, and to this day I am not sure I helped her. I remember she kept saying, "hurry," followed by a "too late, he is already gone."

I believe God does things for a reason, which is why I believe Amy was made to be a part of this family. I am blessed to know Amy but even more blessed to be able to say I am, in Amy's words, her biggest "brudder."

Brian

Villager-11: Brooks siblings

by Candy

To know Amy is to love her. From the very first time that I looked into that sweet, chubby little newborn face, I was in love. I know that that might be an odd thing to say about a sibling, but it is true.

Anyone that looks at Amy sees the obvious. She was born without arms or legs. But when you spend time with Amy, you SEE Her. She is a beautiful, loving, caring, fiercely competitive, determined, optimistic, talented, and loyal-to-a-fault individual with a great sense of humor.

I remember when she was six months old in a hospital for special needs children. My mother was asking for little arms for Amy so that she could move around toys on her special table and chair.

Mom wanted Amy the opportunity to progress like any other "normal" child. The doctor looked at my mother and said, "I don't understand why you would want arms for her. She probably won't be able to use them. In fact, she will probably need to be propped in the corner so that she can sit up."

I remember, very clearly, my mom telling the doctor that "not only will Amy be able to sit without aid, she will be able to walk, and she will get the arms that I am asking for."

Needless to say, we left that doctor both angry and determined that Amy will be able to accomplish all that my mother had professed. With Amy's competitive nature, pure determination, and of course, GOD's help, she surpassed all of those milestones.

I truly believe that GOD placed Amy in our family. I am thankful that HE saw fit to allow me to call her sister and friend.

Candy

Villager-III: Brooks siblings

by Myia

What is there to say about Amy? Plenty! She is awesome! She is a talented artist; has been all of her life. She is the webmaster. Have a problem with your computer, she will fix it. She LOVES the Pens. She has the funniest little squeal when the puck comes close to the net. Never give her a piece of gum and then ask her to speak in public. The rate of speed she can chew while talking, is phenomenal. The speed is only matched if she has gum at a hockey game.

She cries when an extra jalapeno pepper gets into her nachos-n-cheese bite. She is an inspiration. She is determined and strong willed. Never tell her she can't do something, she will prove you wrong.

She is honest. She sees the good in people. She can be hurt, although it will never show to you. She's not quick to share her feelings, but trust me, when she has you for a friend, it means it's friends to the end. She is a daredevil. She will try anything.

She's beautiful, but she won't believe you if you tell her. She has a great sense of humor. If you pulled one over on her, prepare to get paid back in full. She loves her dog, Logic; the two are inseparable. She has overcome a lot in her life. She goes at everything head on. If one way doesn't work, she WILL find another way. She is strong and a fighter. She amazes me constantly.

She is Amy, my sister, my friend. I can find many words to describe her to you, but I can't find the words to get across to you just how deep and how much I love her. There just aren't words for it.

Myia

Villager-IV: Brooks siblings

by Noah

How do you look up to someone who is only two feet tall? Let me tell you how.

You see, it all started when I was ten years old. My parents were foster parents, and my mother's gift was her ability to care for babies with special care requirements.

Little did I know that it meant, one day, having a little sister without arms and legs. Wow, I thought I had seen it all at the ripe age of ten, but it was only the beginning.

I didn't know quite what to make of Amy, but the doctors sure thought they had it pegged. The list of things they said my sister could or would never do was as long as my arm (pun intended).

They were sure Amy would never sit up on her own, never roll over on her own, she would never be able to get around. She couldn't feed herself, take a bath, brush her teeth, comb her hair, or even do her own make-up.

Boy, those doctors couldn't have been more wrong!

When Amy was three or four, I remember thinking I want Amy to be able to get to the second floor of our house without having anyone carry her upstairs. That day sticks out for me more than any as the day I began to look up to my two-foot tall younger sister. Amy was game for most things, so I knew I wouldn't have to do much convincing to get her to try to climb those steps on her own. We started out slow because I wasn't quite sure how to help her accomplish it. I had her put her rear end on the first step and pull herself up with her arm and her chin on the next step. As you can imagine, this was a long tough, exhausting (both physically and mentally) task for Amy.

I just remember encouraging her and telling her she could do it and quite honestly I wasn't going to let her quit until she had reached the top. After two grueling hours, success! I remember looking at her at the top of those steps thinking that she looked larger than life. I remember yelling for my mom to come see what Amy did. The photo that my mom took of her at the top of those steps is still one of my favorites to this very day.

Years have gone by, and Amy is now in grade school. I am in high school. I remember my mother wanting school to be as normal as possible for Amy. My mom asked if I could drive down to the elementary school when I had study hall to help Amy take gym class. Well, I have to admit my first motivation to do it was the fact that I got to drive to school, so I would make it to her gym class in time. Well, the answer to if I would help her was a resounding yes; I got to drive to school. I remember the first day of gym, thinking, What the heck am I going to do with Amy?

Well, I thought, the kids are doing pushups, so I will have Amy do those. Next came sit ups, which actually came naturally to Amy. And last, but not least, came the chin-ups. I tell you what, if you want to freak some people out, put a girl that has no arms on a chin-up bar—and sit back and watch the reactions. That day, everyone was looking up to my two foot tall sister.

Webster's dictionary defines "remarkable" as attracting notice, as being unusual or extraordinary. Most people would think that Amy is remarkable because she can do all of these things without arms and legs. I think that my sister is remarkable because she has a drive and tenacity to do things that I have never seen in anyone.

The word "quit" is not in her vocabulary.

The thing that I look up to my sister the most for is her incredible faith. I truly believe that Amy coming to our family was not by chance; it truly was a divine appointment. She has an inner strength that comes from only one place, God.

So I ask, how can someone look up to someone who is only two feet tall? I invite you to learn more about my sister, and then you can answer the question for yourself.

Noah

Amy's Rebuttal

My goodness! That was all a bit sappy, wasn't it?

I found it quite humbling that my siblings would go behind my back and devise a scheme to write such honorable things about me. And without giving me a chance to defend myself!

Using adjectives like "amazing," "sweet," "talented," and "remarkable,"… Just who did they think they were talking about, anyway? I didn't even recognize the person.

They obviously don't know Amy as well as they claim to.

Regardless, they surprised me with that. "Shocked" would more accurately describe it.

I have to admit that I cried when I read their pages.

Did you cry also?

If you did, you probably have some deep emotional issues to work through.

In the meantime, I hope you continue reading.

Turn the page and let's see what happens next, shall we?

16

Child's Play

Monkey arms and duck feet are not the things of a typical childhood, but that's where mine began. The spoon attachment and banana arm is as far back as my memory goes. Some of it is a blur; some is sharp and vivid.

I remember when I'd sit and play with baby dolls, doing their hair and dressing them. That's what little girls do. But my doll play was different. For one thing, I did it with the use of the rubber hook on my banana arm.

I also recruited my nephew, Wade. He would reach up and take the dolls off the shelf for me. And whether he liked it or not, I got him to help me change their clothes and give them their baths. If I felt he didn't wash the dolls well enough, I made him do it over until they were nice and clean.

But these weren't plastic dolls; they had white cloth bodies. Wade's help came with a warning from me that he couldn't get the white portion of the doll wet or it would turn black and smelly.

In the end, Wade did a pretty good job cleaning my dolls, and I probably should come clean with him. As far as he knew, he was helping me. He didn't realize we were just playing dolls together.

I loved baby dolls—Wade not so much—and I played with them longer than most girls and for a much greater duration than Wade ever did.

When people would make comments about me being too old for dolls, I replied that it would make me a better mom someday.

Climbing in and out of confined spaces was another indoor activity that I enjoyed when I was little, and I always tried new and different ways to do it.

Blending in with my surroundings

Found a cozy spot to read

There were also times that I enjoyed a fair amount of outdoor play. Outside, away from my dolls, I loved going scary fast. Sometimes it was on the back of Wade's Big Wheel. I'd hook my little arms over his shoulders, and he would take off down the sidewalk at full speed.

They see us rollin'...they hatin'

Look, Mom, no hands!

Mom was also a speed donor to my childhood activities. She would tie a rope to the back of our skateboard, and I'd ride it down my wheelchair ramp. As I neared the base of the ramp, Mom used the rope to slow my momentum. She'd then bring me to a stop on the sidewalk.

When we did this, Mom always offered a fair warning to the neighbors: "If you see an unidentified object go flying over your house, it's only Amy because I didn't get her stopped in time."

With the situation left in the hands of two silly females, anything was possible. One miscalculation in Mom's cat-like reflexes, one little hiccup with her bullet-fast reaction time, and I could have taken a self-guided aerial tour of the neighborhood. As fun as that might have been, it didn't happen.

Though I was no longer using the duck feet (which left me mathematically and measurably two feet shorter), and though I wasn't actually using the walker Dad designed, the walker hadn't been officially retired. There was still good mileage on it and plenty of fun to be had by eventually substituting it for the skateboard—but without Mom or her safety rope. I'd ride the walker down the ramp, hoist it over my shoulder, carry it back up, and ride it down again.

Carrying the walker up the ramp—workin' out those shoulder muscles

I came in a fun-sized package, and I've always liked to have fun. This included roller skating on our back porch, having put my skates on just like everyone else—one hip at a time. To do this I'd steady myself against the porch chair and step onto the skates. I then pushed off and scooted around.

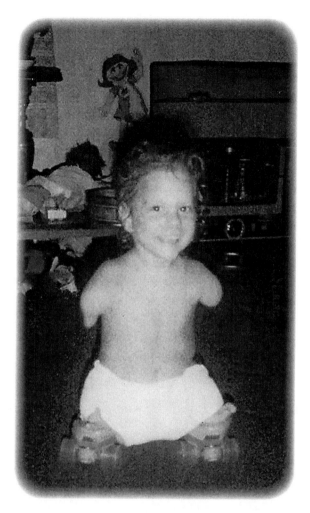

I got a brand new pair of roller skates...

It was something I had a lot of fun with, being silly and making people laugh. Was I a circus clown or an acrobat? I really wasn't sure. I knew I wasn't a good skater and that I'd never earn a spot on any lady's Roller Derby squad, but my performance proved to be quite entertaining for others.

Sometimes I jumped rope with my niece, Brianna. She would tie one end of the rope to the porch banister and twirl the other end for me to jump. When it was Brianna's turn, I twirled for her by holding the rope between my chin and my shoulder.

Believe it or not, there was a time in my childhood when I could do cartwheels too.

Well…half cartwheels.

They were small wheels.

And small carts.

People would probably pay good money to see that now.

I remember Dad built a swing for me and hung it from the roof of the back porch. It consisted of a board with a strip of carpet stapled to it and a chain fastened to the four corners.

When I wasn't on the back porch jumping rope or riding down my wheelchair ramp, I could often be found on that swing. I'd lean my belly against it and walk it up as high as I could go, and then I'd flop further onto it and let it swing me back and forth.

I would also lay on it and push myself in a circular pattern to twist the chain as many times as possible. And then, I'd let it unwind, spinning me around and around like a helicopter blade.

I've been dizzy ever since.

As I grew, Dad raised the swing a few chain links at a time, and I probably got more use out of it than he had ever anticipated. Sometimes I would lay on the swing and just fall asleep.

Just a swingin'

As a kid, I also loved bouncing on our trampoline. I could do that all day long, and that's what worried Mom. With no legs to absorb the shock and lessen the impact, she was concerned that my incessant jumping would cause harm to my lower back.

Because of those worries I had to give up the trampoline, which I hated having to do. But I made the best of it; I traded my trampoline time for the Richard Simmons movement.

Again it was Wade and me. We danced to videos from *Richard Simmons' Sweatin' to the Oldies* like nobody's business. (I'm sure Wade will appreciate me preserving these memories so we can share them with his grandkids someday.)

My favorite dance partner

Wade and I have always had fun quoting movies lines. It's something that we still do. One time, Brianna and I got him to act out a scene from the Disney pirate movie *Hook*.

In the film, there was a wooden "Boo Box" used for punishment. The box had a small door on the top, and when the offender was placed inside, live scorpions were dropped onto him.

How could a kid resist the reenactment of such a scene, especially with a willing participant like Wade? Given the fact that we had a tank of hermit crabs and a large cardboard box on our back porch, it was all too tempting.

We named ours the "Booboo box," and I persuaded Wade to climb inside. After he did, Brianna and I proceeded to drop the hermit crabs onto him. It didn't take long for Wade to let out a scream. Brianna insisted he was only fooling us, so we didn't release him right away.

We added more crabs instead.

When we did finally open the box, Wade had a crab attached to him. Apparently, our booboo box experiment was affective because he did receive a booboo that day.

These make up some of the fond childhood memories that I cherish. In reflection, we can dismiss the monkey arms and duck feet. With remembrances of baby dolls, and jump ropes, hermit crabs, and mischief— maybe mine was just another typical childhood.

Wade helped me practice gymnastics, too

17

Special Olympian

The one thing that wasn't all too normal about the majority of my childhood—compared to most kids—was the excursion I had to take to simply go to bed at night.

It began by inching my way up sixteen steps to the second floor, which is where all the bedrooms are.

I think I can

I was three, maybe four when Noah taught me how to successfully climb the staircase. He also developed and demonstrated a good way for me to safely slide down to the bottom. We spent two hours perfecting the entire routine, and I credit him for that accomplishment. From there, climbing up and sliding down became a game for me.

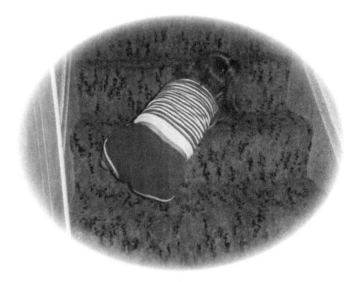

I think I can

I know I can

I did!

As for falling, I figured that out on my own; Noah never had to help me with it. Not only did I independently discover the amazing effects of gravity, I did it with the grace and style of a qualified Olympian.

Like most of my other blunders, it was all self-taught, with no special training required.

Though you might consider me a dope, I can honestly say that I've never used any performance-enhancing drugs of any mix or variety. Of more importance is that you'll never see me appear on a television talk show to recant those statements in an effort to resurrect my stair-falling career.

The truth is that I've never even consumed an energy drink, and I can't tolerate the taste of coffee. Any of those substances would likely cause me to do more stupid things at an accelerated pace, such as plummeting down the same stairs that I had already so proudly conquered.

It happened one morning after I had just awakened. For some reason, I decided to go downstairs unassisted and didn't even bother to tell Mom I was coming. I just went for it.

That's when it happened.

I'm not sure how a person without legs can manage to trip themselves, but I found a way to do it. In hindsight, I probably should have had it patented.

If you're wondering, the answer is yes: I have always performed my own stunts. Thus, I do consider myself a true professional of the consummate variety. It just derives from raw talent—completely unrehearsed, with no green screens or special effects.

No hired stand-in.

No paid actress.

No Hollywood stunt double.

Additionally, I have never employed the use of a safety net or any other source of fall protection—not even a protective layer of bubble wrap or a barrier of "caution" tape.

On the morning of the fall, I had intended to fully adhere to all proper mountaineering procedures on my decent toward the breakfast table. But when it came down to it, I lacked the appropriate climbing/rappelling attire.

It so happened that I was wearing those pajamas that zip at the bottom like a gym bag. This proved to be the contributing factor, causing me to topple, end-over-end, like a dropped football.

Another Fumble!

All the way to the bottom I went.

However, it really wasn't as thoughtless and uncontrolled as it might sound. I quickly transformed it into a display of elegance and dexterity.

I had a strong takeoff.

Proper form.

Nice tuck.

Perfect roll.

Decent hang time between bounces.

I knew I didn't stick the landing as nicely as I should have. Olympic-caliber judges would probably deduct a point for banking myself off the wall on dismount. But with high marks for good technique and artistic expression, I think it would have evened out. I also think I should have made the front of a Wheaties box for it.

Here's a puzzle solver for you: if you've ever wondered why you don't see professional climbers wearing zip-up pajamas it's because of me. But I haven't figured out why gymnasts don't wear them.

Overall, I'd say I scored a solid 9.2 or better.

I realize it doesn't equal an eighteen-year-old Art Shamsky hitting a homer on his first at-bat as a pro ball player, but my endeavor wasn't too shabby for a rookie attempt at a medal.

Not only was it an indication of my superb athleticism, it also testified to how fortunate I've always been. Mom simply picked me up, dusted me off, and sent me on my way.

Anyone else might have easily broken an arm or a leg.

18

Phantom Protection

For those of you who may have been disappointed that there wasn't a test at the conclusion of chapter three, dig out your pencils.

Here's a question for you:

If you were required to do so, which would you choose between these two possible circumstances?

> *A) Being born without limbs?*

> *B) Having perfectly good limbs that would later be lost?*

Good luck!

I know it's a toughie, but you only have ten seconds, so don't dillydally.

Which would you circle?

Choice A?

Don't over think it.

How is choice B looking?

Do you have an answer?

Eyes on your own paper, please.

Time's up.

Pencils down.

Sorry.

How'd you do with that?

You might think that it was a trick question. I don't believe it was, but there probably isn't an actual right or wrong answer. Your opinion is as good as anyone else's, and each of you get credit for trying.

Concerning the first scenario, it's probably something you've never had to consider. In all fairness, you're possibly thinking that you've never even heard of *Tetra-phoco-whatever-it's-called* until reading this book. So, it's highly likely that you've never imagined what's it's like to be born without limbs.

Realizing this now to be a rare possibility, you may consider it to be the better of the two adoptions. In my case, it's all I've known. I've adapted the best I can, from birth up. You might think that would be best.

Unfortunately, the second scenario isn't as rare as we'd all like it to be. Various wars and hostilities have forced us to imagine that which is unimaginable. These brutal conflicts have mass-produced a horrific tragedy and exported its product in bulk to our country and to the lands of our allies.

Scores of limbless soldiers are the result.

As atrocious as this has been, some may choose it—choice B—over the other. Having experienced physical wholesomeness and enjoyed the benefits of human normalcy, they may conclude that it's better to have had and to have lost than to never have had at all.

That's what makes this unusual question so difficult.

Through it all, you'd probably assume that the first is the only scenario that would fit me, and I guess it is. However, the summer of 2011 brought us the true and tragic story of a soldier to whom I could also relate. Some might not think so at first, but as we carry it through the next chapter, you'll catch the similarity.

You may have missed it when the story initially aired because it mirrored so many others.

It began as a repeat of occurrences:

Army veteran is deployed to the Middle East...

Explosive device causes traumatic amputation...

Soldier survives and returns home to recover...

It could have gone passed like a rerun, but it wasn't a rerun; it was the broadcasting of yet another disturbing occurrence of war.

In this story, the soldier lost his entire left leg, part of his hip, and nearly as much on the right side. After more than two grueling years of medical follow-ups and painful rehabilitation, the man was finally able to return home for good.

You'd think a day out with family and friends would do him some good. He deserved that. This soldier had sacrificed greatly for his country. His body had been thrown to the outer rim of existence, and he spilled his blood over the very edge of eternity. Yet, he courageously clawed his way back.

He was highly disciplined, a stern, well trained warrior.

A fighter and a survivor.

Battle tested and tough as nails.

Amongst the best of the best, he had suffered the worst of the worst, and he was extremely fortunate to be alive.

When the armor-penetrating warhead struck, the man bled so profusely that he suffered severe brain damage from the blood loss and oxygen deprivation. He experienced two strokes and had been in a coma for several weeks while being treated amongst a chain of hospitals.

Rebuilding his life and reclaiming his abilities seemed impossible, but he was doing it, remarkably. Relearning everything from how to talk and feed himself, along with adjusting to life without his legs, he fought as relentlessly in the hospitals as he had on the battlefields.

And he was winning.

At this point the worst was behind him. He had endured the pains and beaten the odds.

The man was fearless, and after everything he had experienced, he should have had no further worries. Only good things should have awaited him.

When he slid into the seat of the roller coaster at the upstate New York amusement park, he was joyful and carefree. He was excited. He was anticipating a momentary thrill, a quick and passing distraction from his new and cruel reality.

Having already suffered more than anyone should, what harm could possibly come his way? What dangers could now confront him?

From there he would continue his day and further his life. He would go on to enjoy his loved-ones, his kids, his friends, his relatives. He would savor life and appreciate the world around him.

At least that's how his story should have gone.

He should have wheeled safely into the sunset without any future concerns, but that isn't what would actually happen.

As the roller coaster neared the end of its ride, the soldier was tragically ejected.

One may consider the various elements of the Laws of Physics at work in this disaster, but a simplified rendition does exist. An abbreviated interpretation is evident, and I've learned it by experience.

You see, I discovered something, long ago: a lap belt is rendered ineffective if it has no lap to hold.

19

Law of Motion

The first of three Laws of Motion states: *the velocity of a body remains constant unless the body is acted upon by an external force.*

Hence: *a body at rest tends to stay at rest, and a body in motion tends to stay in motion…*

God invented that.

Sir Isaac Newton discovered it.

My family proved it, assisted by a stranger.

I was five years old when it happened.

Like the soldier in the previous pages, I had the anticipation of continued life and health ahead of me. The sky was blue, and the smell of fresh doughnuts wafted through the air.

When I was three, Dr. Alexander had strongly suggested that I attend preschool. In fact he ordered it, informing Mom that I needed to go and that she needed to let me go.

Thus, my pre-K attendance was prescribed as much for her as it was for me—so she could have a short break and I could get out of the house more often and out from under her over-protectiveness.

At this time in my life, I had completed the two years of that recommendation at a rate of two hours a day, two days a week, at a local church preschool facility.

With that behind me, I was soon to be promoted; my entrance into kindergarten was rapidly approaching.

There was also something else behind me—behind *us*—and it too was rapidly approaching, but none of us were aware of it. Everything was normal, quiet, and peaceful.

From the back seat, I keenly eyed the doughnut shop that appeared through the window. Dad was at the wheel, Mom was riding shotgun, and Noah was strapped in next to me.

Life was good, all was well, and that doughnut shop seemed warmly inviting.

That was when our test of Physics was inadvertently conducted. It occurred at an intersection, beneath a traffic light.

It was a red one.

Bold and solid.

It wasn't pink.

It wasn't negotiable.

It was red, all the way to the core, with no grey areas.

No room for vague interpretations.

Its meaning is understood by all peoples and languages, but the message is often lost to those who are affected by drunkenness or anger. Stirring both together is a toxic recipe waiting to create a hazardous spill. That's essentially what happened on this particular afternoon.

The bodies at rest were those of our family Oldsmobile and a pickup truck directly behind us.

Stopped.

Waiting.

Completely at rest.

The object in motion that would "act upon" these bodies appeared in the form of a speeding automobile operated by an irate and inebriated motorist. The driver had pulled out of a restaurant a ways back and floored it after fighting with his girlfriend.

Energy, mass, hostility, and impairment—it all rushed forward, unobstructed and uninhibited, traveling at a constant velocity.

There was then the sudden impedance of that harmonic movement. The induction of it was quick and harsh, and the impact was violent.

Smashing metal.

Exploding glass.

Intense fright.

Though I had no idea of what had happened, we had become the third element of a three-vehicle, rear-end collision. The angry and speeding drunk driver had slammed into the pickup behind us, forcing it into our car. All I knew was that one minute I was thinking about doughnuts and the next I was draped over the edge of the back seat—upside down, face to the floor.

Like in the story of the soldier, I had been torn from my seatbelt and ejected forward. I was terrified and screaming my head off.

In the chaos, Mom initially thought my cries were coming from under the front seat, as if I was lodged beneath it. Soon after, I was in her arms, being consoled and inspected for damage.

Everything was a blur of fear and confusion, as everyone climbed out of the mangled vehicles. For the most part, we all seemed to be okay. The driver of the pickup and everyone was standing around. Except for the drunk; he was sprawled out on the ground, uninjured but babbling incoherently.

By then I had stopped crying. Mostly I was wide-eyed with shock. I was injured, but none of us knew it at the time, not even me. The only thing that seemed to hurt was when a police officer walked up and asked, "Is the baby alright?"

For a moment I forgot about the trauma we had just experienced. This respected man in uniform had now added practical insult to my personal injury.

I was not a baby!

I was going on six years old!

He was a policeman; didn't he know I was going into kindergarten?

With our test of Physics concluded and with things settled at the accident scene, Brian came and drove the four of us to the hospital to get checked out.

Dad was hurt with his herniated disc.

Mom had whiplash.

Noah was fine.

The hospital wasn't quite sure of what to do with me. That sounds eerily familiar, doesn't it?

A Dr. Johnstone examined me and studied my x-rays, but he couldn't make a specific diagnosis. He was confident I had no fractures or lacerations.

Beyond that, he was puzzled by what he was seeing and unsure of what he was looking for because he didn't know how I looked prior to the crash.

What was normal for me and what wasn't?

He was dealing with too much of the unknown. My parts are as miscellaneous as they are mysterious. Everything is varied and mismatched.

They say everyone has a skeleton in their closet. If that's so, and if you have any extra pieces lying around, I'll be glad to accept a donation.

I have a semi-normal hip bone on the right side, only a partially formed one on the left, and no ball and socket on either. My muscles have also shaped themselves accordingly.

The congenital formation of my right hip is actually worse than the left, but the accident injured my left hip. So, in a weird and unpleasant way, I'm balanced out; they are now both equally bad, but the left side gives me the most discomfort.

Through it all, Dr. Johnstone couldn't tell what was common to my birth diagnosis and what might have been crash related. The poor guy could hardly determine which end was up.

His poking and prodding seemed to indicate that I did have muscle injuries and ligament damage, but he didn't know what to do about it. He released me, untreated, hoping I'd heal and recover naturally.

We all went home with the three of us in need of a good dose of healing. As is often true in life though, things got worse before we got better.

Further injury would be added to our family over the coming year, with Dad being out of work and having to sell his truck. He and Mom had a long, painful recovery, which I wasn't completely aware of at that time and age.

I certainly became conscious of my own injuries, however.

A few days after the crash, pain surfaced in my back and left hip. I was a kid with things to do, so I tried to ignore it. There was no room for an injury timeout. With fun to be had, I played through it as much as possible.

The pain often grew to become quite excruciating and constant. It seemed to linger forever before eventually lessening to a tolerable level, but it never completely dissipated.

Oftentimes, I'd have to stop what I was doing and go to Mom for a quick massage so I could continue playing. The pain would temporarily subside, and off I'd go again.

There were many times at night when I was in misery and couldn't sleep or find any physical comfort. This was likely due to me overdoing it—further aggravating the injuries—when I played throughout the day.

When the worst of the aching flare-ups occurred, Mom would place a pillow under my throbbing hip to alleviate some of the pressure. It helped a little, but it seemed that as soon as I dozed off, I'd slide off the pillow and scream out with pain again.

Yet, these nighttime episodes didn't reduce my daytime activities. I carried on as much as ever. The main and lingering difference was that I moved a little slower, and I walked with a limp.

I still do.

At the really bad times—of which there were many—I'd be confined to my bed, unable to do anything. When I could move, I certainly didn't set any new land speed records. In fact, I probably couldn't have activated a motion sensor if I was sitting on one.

I had always traveled at a leisurely pace as it was, but pain flare-ups slowed me even more. So much so that if I had gone any slower, I would have been going in reverse.

I'm not sure if there is anything that moves slower than a land snail, but if you can think of something, that has often been me.

A house plant perhaps?

I'm sure if I had challenged Mom's potted palm tree to a race across the living room, I would have easily lost.

All of this is a permanent memento, a childhood keepsake, a reminder of how one person's careless actions can affect the well-being of another.

The insurance company of the man who hit us did eventually cover our medical expenses and the repair costs for our car. After getting the car fixed, Dad came up with a seatbelt improvement idea, which he presented to Nemours/Alfred I. duPont Hospital for Children, in Wilmington, Delaware.

By that time, our beloved Dr. Alexander had transferred to that facility, and we followed him there like remedial groupies.

Dad's intent was for me to have a U-shaped safety belt that would be permanently bolted in place. The design was approved, and duPont manufactured it for us.

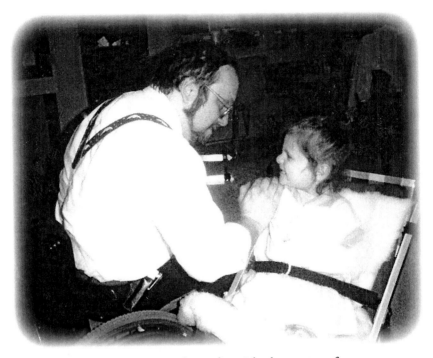

Arm-wrestling Dr. Alexander...I let him win, of course.

The belt came up and over my shoulders, and the rear seatbelt laced through it, creating an H-type harness. My parents felt it was yet inadequate but better than the standard factory seatbelt assembly, which of course are designed for whole-body passengers. We could only hope it would help counter the natural rules of Physics should another accident occur.

Thankfully, we never had to truly test its sufficiency.

The entire accident ordeal was awful.

But consider the soldier who was ejected from the roller coaster—he died in that fall.

His story serves as a sobering reminder that, no matter how bad your day has been and how traumatic your experience was, someone else has had one that's worse. That might also prove to be a universal law, someday.

20

Off and Rolling

lthough we had the unplanned, unpleasant details of the accident to deal with—Mom and Dad especially—other things began coming together, and my life was beginning to move in a new direction and by a different, more improved method.

When I wasn't being carried in the arms of my parents or Brian, I was pushed in a large umbrella-type stroller, and then buckled into the back seat of the car. I was completely dependent in that regard, but those factors changed shortly before I entered first grade.

Again, it was Dr. Alexander who came to the rescue; he saw to it that I got my first wheelchair. The unit was custom made in England. It was battery powered, of course, and the seat lowered all the way to the floor, which made it easy for me to climb into on my own. It could also be raised enough to allow me to sit at the proper height of tables and countertops.

That particular model type was called a Turbo, which sounds much faster than it actually was. When I saw that it wasn't equipped with a wheelie bar or a parachute, I immediately realized drag racing would be out of the question. But it was showroom clean, with that permeating new-car smell, and I was happy to have it.

Conveniently, my parents had a large wooden porch built onto the back of the house. The work was done by a contractor friend of ours, Mark Hubert. The structure measures 336 square feet.

Those are a lot of feet no matter what their shape. When you don't have any, you're not too fussy about whether they are square, round, or oblong.

Feet are feet, right?

All I know is that I was always partial to the back porch, and the best part of it was the adjoining ramp. Not only was it where I did a lot of playing, it was also where I learned to drive my wheelchair.

For operating abilities, I was also issued a pair of passive arms. I call them mannequin arms because that's what they look like. They consisted of flesh-tone hollow acrylic, human-shaped limbs. My hands were a pair of not-so-fashionable metal hooks. These hooks were held in the closed position with rubber bands. I quickly learned how to open them by flexing my shoulders.

As for the wheelchair, we didn't have anyone to teach me how to formally operate it, but we're not formal-type people anyhow.

The thing was simply delivered to our home one day, and there it was. It probably came with a set of instructions, but no one ever reads that stuff. Mom and Dad guided me, and we figured it out on our own.

I had to turn it on with a white button. There was also a red one that beeped for whatever reason—possibly to warn nearby pedestrians that I was on the loose. To steer I'd maneuver a joy stick with my hook by pushing or pulling it with movements from my shoulder.

Yeah, okay. Whatever. Outta my way. Here I go!

It was all pretty easy, and I got it immediately. Grabbing the controls, I began weaving in and out and around everyone and everything on the back porch.

As great as it was to take possession of the wheelchair, it would not become an everyday, all-day amenity. Essentially, it was for outdoor use only, my own private mode of conveyance solely designated for public transportation.

It was like it had come with one of those "Don't try this in your home" warnings, and there was a good and practical reason for that.

The back porch was the only place on our property where I could use my wheelchair because our interior doorways were too narrow to accommodate its width. Once inside, it was parked, and I'd have to amble around the house as before.

Licensed to drive

This remains true today.

With ownership of the wheelchair came the question of how we'd best transport it. Fortunately, around the same time, we received a modest settlement from the collision, though the man's insurance company had initially fought it.

Apparently, they felt we shouldn't have been sitting in their client's path when he sped off in a drunken rage, with the intent of blowing a stale red light.

Life can be funny like that, I suppose.

When the check finally came, my parents used it to purchase a pre-owned and well-used van that would nicely accommodate me and my new ride.

The van didn't have a power lift or a ramp. So, Dad sprang into action as always. Despite his relentless aches and pains, he built a set of wooden ramps for it.

The ramps had to be stowed, pulled out, and put into place, one at a time, but they and the van served their purpose. It was all a big upgrade from what we'd had and from how we'd done things prior.

Inside the van, the wheelchair was secured with tie-downs on each of the four wheels, but there remained an imminent threat that I'd be thrown from it without a better seatbelt.

To prevent that from happening again, Dad returned to duPont where a harness was constructed similar to the one they had made for our car.

With that I'd be all set.

Dad wasn't the only one who'd experience life on wheels.

There I was—in a Turbo wheelchair, prosthetic arms, and a roomy van. The school bell would soon ring, and whether or not the world around me was prepared, I was ready to roll.

21

Halls of Learning

As with any kid, to officially enter school was a milestone for me; although it was really more of a beginning than an actual marked achievement.

Preschool had passed without effort—mostly in a blur of tears and in a haze of sand. The only things I remember of those two years was sometimes crying when Mom dropped me off and then playing in the sandbox when I got over it.

During that time, I was also drawn to arts and crafts. My teacher, Miss Theresa, said I always got right in there with the rest of the class whenever they did art projects, but I don't especially remember that. I do remember enjoying the sandbox though, and I played in it as much as they'd allow.

Kindergarten consisted of the usual things—the complexities of alphabets and numbers and a fascination with colors and shapes.

It also included a lot of Happy Meals!

Of course, these weren't part of the school lunch menu or something that was on my daily list of mother-approved snack options, but I had them anyway.

They were provided by a kind, older gentleman whose name I don't recall. He transported me in a school van. Mom would push me in the stroller and buckle me into the front passenger seat, where I felt very comfortable chatting, nonstop, to the driver.

He was the grandfatherly type, who probably would have been as content in a wooden rocking chair as he was in the driver's seat.

I was quite rambunctious and talkative at that age, and I had no reluctances to disclosing the things that were of utmost importance to me. In so doing—as most five-year-olds would likely do—I declared my allegiance to McDonald's Happy Meals.

The man then started bringing me those for my ride home from Kindergarten. It quickly became an every-Friday ritual. Mom would constantly tell him to not get them for me, but he insisted. He said that I liked them and that he liked getting them for me. So, he did.

Mom had either lost the argument or had finally given up, and I continued to get the Happy Meals. That was one of my fondest memories of kindergarten.

However, for me kindergarten contained something more. That something was actually a "someone," and she was a Godsend.

It was there, in kindergarten, that I met Elaine Myers. She was "Mrs. Myers" to me and the other students because she was a teaching aide. Mrs. Myers and I became extremely close as she was assigned to look after me throughout all of my school years, until I graduated high school.

This was an incredible task, performed unwaveringly by a wonderful person. Though she had additional assignments and responsibilities with helping other teachers and students, Mrs. Myers assisted me wherever necessary.

I wasn't enrolled in private education or in any establishment for special needs students, which was one of the many ways that my parents helped to normalize my life.

Because of them and the dedication of Mrs. Myers, I was able to attend and complete regular public school that had no particular accommodations or comfort items for anyone who might be considered handicapped.

I had my wheelchair and the short school bus on which I was transported, and in many of my classes, I had a special desk that sort of wrapped around the sides of me. Other than that, there were no special provisions—except for Mrs. Myers. For thirteen years she was an extreme and absolute blessing to me.

Together we reinvented and redefined the buddy system.

Her assistance was more prevalent during my elementary years where she sometimes took notes for me during class. She also accompanied me between classes, helped me with my books, got my lunch, and offered me assistance in the restroom. At the end of the school day, she then made sure I got onto the bus okay.

Mrs. Myers wasn't always in class with me as if she had to shadow my every move, but she would always come when requested. I hated to ask for help, but when I was sure I needed it, my teacher would page Mrs. Myers over the public address system—and she emerged without fail.

In my 7th-grade year, she was a tremendous help. It was then that I matriculated into high school, as us Avalon kids and those from Bellevue merged and converged on the building of Northgate Jr./Sr. High School.

As its name suggests, the facility is an amalgamation of all those grade levels. Two schools in one building, to double the pleasure of the whole education experience.

Or something like that.

Identical to the mascot of a rival NHL team—located a good distance on a north-left vector from Pittsburgh—Northgate is home of the Flames. This would probably explain the excessive and untimely fire drills we endured there. I suppose those were intended to double our pleasure as well.

After all, who doesn't love a good fire drill? You have to appreciate the customary practice of conducting them on the coldest, windiest, most rainy days of the school year. One could only assume the logic was that the elements would snuff out the imaginary flames in our hair and clothing.

It was only during those fire drills that the halls would become completely hallow, with all the bodies of the student body huddled outside in a substantial wad.

The interesting thing about a Northgate crowd was that the bigger it was, the more people showed up to be a part of it. This was most noticeable during school assemblies and fire drills. From my perspective, these human jumblings were packed with strangers and layered with intimidation.

Compared to most, Northgate is a rather small school. Yet, it didn't seem very small to me, especially when I first arrived. I was blended with the youngest of the students entering the high school, and I was the smallest among them. When you're my size, everything seems bigger; little schools have a way of becoming sprawling universities.

Getting off a short bus and rolling into the place was quite unsettling. The school was loud, and everyone moved faster than what I was accustomed to.

It was like a tornado had spun through the area, gathered everyone from the age of twelve to eighteen, stuffed them through the school doors, and swirled them about. And they continued to swirl, stuck together in a particular camaraderie that I wasn't actually a part of. It seemed everyone there knew each other, but it somehow didn't include me.

It was of no added benefit that I was extremely shy at that time. Far behind me was the image of the chipper kindergartener who proudly received weekly Happy Meals. To say I was self-conscious is an understatement. I barely knew any of the students in my classes, and I felt lost and isolated against the crowds.

In Pre-K I was just another dust muncher in the sandbox. In kindergarten I seemed to fit in so well that, even then, I didn't understand it.

Our friend and neighbor, Chris, recalls a brief exchange she and I had about that one day. Apparently there isn't anything funny on television because it's something she and Mom still laugh about after all these years.

I had just come in from my first day of kindergarten. As she often would do, Miss Chris had dropped in for a visit, and she encountered me in the kitchen. With her back pressed against the refrigerator, she slid into a squatting position to put herself at eye-level with me.

"Hi, Amy," she said. "How was school today?"

"I don't understand something," I replied.

Miss Chris probably thought I was baffled by some of the classroom material or school procedure. Instead, I told her, "I don't know why nobody asked me why I'm so short."

I guess I expected it back then, and I welcomed it. Yet, no one seemed to notice. Later on, I didn't want them to.

By the time I reached junior high school, a feeling of awkwardness accompanied me. It could have been that I created a level of awkwardness for some of the other students as well. Maybe it wasn't popular to hang out with a student in a wheelchair.

Thus, it took me a long time to settle in and acquire friends. At least it seemed that way. The funny thing is that I think most everyone liked me. Anytime I got the courage to ask someone for help, they were happy to give it. I can see that now, but back then I couldn't.

Sometimes they even helped when I didn't ask. A boy by the name of Peter offers a good example. He and I had never spoken and for no particular reason other than my own introversion. One day Peter surprised me with an act of kindness that I've never forgotten.

Before the bell rang, I motored into class and directed my wheelchair toward my desk. Peter then entered the room. In a kind, gentlemanly fashion, he slid my desk in front of me so I could easily drive under it.

I said thank you, and he simply took his seat. Those are the only two words I've ever spoken to him, but I've always appreciated that caring act.

After parking beneath my desk and raising my chair to the proper height, I just sat there. For one thing, I had no one to help get me set up for class, and I didn't want to ask Peter for any further assistance. So, I sat and waited, feeling grateful for what he had already done for me.

When my friend, Maria, came in, she retrieved my things from my book bag and got me fully situated.

Class began.

Life went on.

Peter remained an unknown but unforgotten stranger.

I'm sure my circle of friends would have measured a much greater circumference had I put forth more effort. I wish I had done so. Peter, and others like him, would have certainly made that circle more complete.

A constant concern of mine at Northgate was that we had only four minutes to get from one class to the next. This created a persistent challenge. Though Mrs. Myers would come after each class and gather my books, I didn't like maneuvering through the halls with the rest of the students.

Amongst the human congestion, I was convinced I'd run someone over or myself be trampled before each school day was finished. This wasn't due to me being a reckless driver but a nervous one.

As time went on, I began to make some new and close friends— probably because I hadn't run them over. I also wanted to gain more independence and not rely as much on Mrs. Myers. So, the teachers permitted me and a friend to leave class a few minutes early to avoid the holiday rush.

This allowed us time to each go to our lockers, and my friend could escort me to my next class and get herself to her own class, all before the bell rang. This helped reduce my chance of being late. As a self-professed worry wart, tardiness has always been on my list of concerns.

I've forever feared losing a loved-one.

I get creeped out by scary movies.

I'm afraid of heavy storms.

And I stress over being absent or tardy.

It was rare that my friends would be absent or involved with other school activities that caused them to miss class. But I often felt a relentless, underlying apprehension that they wouldn't be there to take me around.

If I had to call for Mrs. Myers she was sure to come, but it meant that I typically had to wait for the bell to ring before setting out. This would again place me amongst the running of the bulls.

Basically, these anxieties remained with me throughout all my school years, high school especially. It wasn't that I was truly afraid per se; I just never wanted to be in the way or impede the foot traffic.

You just can't always trust people with feet, you know?

Therefore, the notion lingered and the questions persisted:

On what day would I become the bug?

On what day would I become the windshield?

Squishing or being squished—neither appealed to me, but both were equally valid possibilities.

I was convinced something undesirable would ensue.

It would only be a matter of time.

22

School of Hard Knocks

Within any gathering of people, you'll encounter those who are the self-appointed pranksters, and in every school, you'll surely meet the elected class clown.

Apparently, these are good paying and well-regarded positions because there seemed to be an overabundance of both of those student categories at Northgate.

Luckily, the reputations of such in my circle were fun-loving and relatively harmless. On more than one occasion, they genuinely assisted me, and on more than one occasion, I had become the object of their diabolical schemes.

I was fortunate to have avoided the casual wedgie and to have been spared the random swirlie, but let's be real: a limbless girl in a wheelchair can be too easy a target to not take aim at once in a while, right?

Some occurrences just happened, some were self-induced, and some were perpetrated by others. Each event contributed to the gaining of some bonus points and the earning of a few gold stars at the school of hard knocks.

Though I'm sure it happened more than twice, I do recall two specific instances where my wheelchair battery died. Once was in fifth grade, and my friend, Dana, volunteered to push me around all day.

Dana was only in fifth grade as well, but she was up to the challenge, and she did it enthusiastically. If she had been tempted to leave me stranded and allow me to be tardy, she never let on. Maybe that would have been too easy or too predictable.

The other time I lost power was in high school, in ninth grade or so. I was in computer class, on the second floor. On that day I didn't have any friends in there who could accompany me to my next class.

I was nervous about it, but I figured I could venture out unassisted. I'd have friends in my next class, which was just a little ways down the hall and around the corner.

I didn't have to stop at my locker to swap books. All I'd have to do is slip into my prosthetic arms, lower my wheelchair, and back out from beneath my desk. I figured I'd be fine if I could only get myself to my next class, but to do so I'd have to gather enough courage to ask someone to open the door for me.

Suddenly, the skies parted above the school. God must have smiled down because the teacher went out abruptly and left the classroom door open. That was my chance to make a quiet, unobtrusive escape. So, I did.

It was a clean get-away.

An open door.

No classroom disruption.

No asking for help.

Piece of cake!

It should have been all downhill from there. In fact, if it literally was, I wouldn't have encountered any problems; gravity and momentum would have done the rest.

As I started down the hall, everything was going well. I'd soon be in a room with some familiar faces and long before the bell rang.

Yep, God was smiling on me.

But wait! Was there a breeze outside? Did cloud cover blow in and block the effectiveness of that smile?

Without warning my chair just stopped moving!

Mrs. Myers wasn't with me.

The halls were completely empty.

There were no curious onlookers.

No Dana to give me a push.

No lost and wondering souls.

No custodian.

No trespassers.

No one!

I had passed the point of common nervousness about half way back, and though my wheelchair had stopped rolling, I felt myself rapidly approaching the on-ramp of panic.

The bell was about to ring, and I had no clue as to what to do or how to survive the eminent stampede.

Hold it! Did the wind pick up again? Was God still smiling?

Apparently so because I suddenly saw an unexpected angel walking toward me.

Well, he wasn't a classic angel. Not the traditional cherubim or seraphim type. He was sort of a modern-day personification of Clarence Oddbody, I suppose. It was actually Mr. Gaetano, the guidance counselor.

Close enough to an angel to me, under the circumstances.

Where I usually had reservation about asking for help with something as basic as a closed door, I miraculously lost that shyness and spilled out the enormities of my problems to Mr. Gaetano.

Much like my dad would do, the man was moved to quick and decisive action. Mr. Gaetano immediately made an announcement for four football players to come meet him in the second floor hallway.

If Dana could push me by herself, anyone could. I tried to tell Mr. Gaetano that I'd only need one person, but he insisted on doing it his way. Next thing I knew I was facing four overgrown varsity football players.

Mr. Gaetano ordered two on either side of me. All four ran and pushed with the synchronized harmony of a bobsled team, and my chair had never moved so fast.

Where is that wheelie bar and parachute when you really need them?

The whole thing would have been humorously reminiscent of my infant football days with Myia and Jenn if I could actually remember back that far. I know God remembered it, and I think that smile of His became a thundering laugh with this particular incident.

Surrounded by these beef-eating, knuckle-dragging jocks, I seemed to have become a football once again. To them, every movable object is a ball, and anyplace is a playing field.

With four guys pushing me in a wheelchair, I was rushed at lightning speed down the entire length of the hallway. As we rounded the corner, I thought I was going to flip sideways and fall out, making me all the more appreciative of seatbelts.

The whole experience was a blast, and I was laughing my head off the entire way.

The guys put me in the elevator and took me downstairs to a classroom where I could stay and do my work for the remainder of the school day. When we got to the first floor, they were having so much fun that they wanted to take me on a run around the school.

Mrs. Myers had apparently been paged or somehow showed up at that time, and she wouldn't allow the guys to take me on the extended high speed excursion. But I didn't hold it against her.

As mentioned earlier, I have always liked going fast. I'd prefer that over a slow pace or a dead battery, anytime.

I recall another school wheelchair incident that was strange and fearful, but I was never sure of its cause. While working a math problem at the chalkboard one day, I caught a whiff of what seemed to be an electrical overload or some type of overheating condition.

Naturally, I assumed it was coming from my wheelchair. Various frightening images and gruesome questions immediately raced through my mind.

Was it going to catch fire?

Could I be blown up?

Eventually, the smell dissipated without incident.

No wheelchair fire.

No classroom explosion.

No radical representation of a true Northgate Flame.

No fire drill.

I never did learn the source of the stench, but I can't deny being scared by it. I now realize that some of my fears were considerably unrealistic, but they seemed perfectly valid at the time.

I also did things that would eventually produce other stressful moments before my years of education would be complete. Occasionally, I'd allow my school friends to drive my chair—meaning they walked beside me and operated the controls. My speed was always set on "high" to keep up with the flow of traffic, and my friends knew that. They also were aware of my obsession with punctuality.

One time, my friend, Emily, was working the controls. She drove me up to the door of a classroom and turned down the speed on my chair to the lowest setting, which is somewhere between "sundial" and "dialup Internet." She then turned off the power and ran off.

I was left there looking through the little window of the classroom door. The students looked out at me as though I was some sort of creeper—and I kind of felt like one.

Dana probably would have never done that. The ironic thing about Emily is that she was Dana's handpicked replacement as a friend for me.

When Dana transferred to a different school, she connected me with her friend, Emily, who then became my friend too. They were both good friends to me, but Dana was a more sincere helper. Emily was mischievous. Dana assisted my immobility, Emily contributed to it.

Her prank of leaving me stranded and abandoned was successful enough that it seemed to demand an encore presentation because she repeated the stunt another time.

However, instead of returning to the scene of the original crime, Emily changed venues and chose a different audience. The second time was in front of the office, which had a full wall of windows from ceiling to floor.

Of course she had to push me right up against the glass, facing inward, before she ran off.

Until I could get powered up and readjust my speed, I again sat there gazing in with the office workers gazing out. It flustered me that I couldn't get away fast enough, but I think it's funny now.

In all this, Emily made a clean get away, but it was in good fun, and there was another time when she seemed to make up for it by literally offering me a helping hand.

A comedian named Mitch Hedberg once said, "It's very dangerous to wave to people you don't know because what if they don't have hands? They'll think you're cocky."

That's an interesting thought. I have been on the receiving end of a few waves over the years but have never thought anyone was being cocky or showing off in any way.

In contrast, what if you are the sender and not the recipient? What do you do if you are a student without arms who wants to raise your hand in class?

Been there, done that, bought the tee shirt.

Okay, before having to come back and edit in the truth, I should rephrase that: I've been there, tried it, and wasn't successful.

There were also no tee shirts to buy.

It was in my senior elective biology class. That room didn't have traditional desks; it had long tables abutted end to end.

I was parked at the back table, bookended by Emily and my niece, Brianna. As usual, I had slid out of prosthetic arms because they serve no function other than driving my wheelchair. They are also too heavy for me to lift into the air if I wanted to raise my hand.

On that day, a student teacher, Ms. Maier, was conducting class on behalf of Mr. Donini. She asked a question, and I knew the answer. So, I raised my little arm.

Being seated in the back of the room and raising what's equivalent to a Popsicle stick, Ms. Maier didn't see it. No one else wanted to answer the question. I kept waving my arm, but I was passed over.

Finally, Emily grabbed my prosthetic arm, held it high in the air, and started waving it around. Ms. Maier couldn't help but to notice that. She also couldn't help but to bust out with laughter. Brianna, Emily, and I all laughed too, as the rest of the class looked around with no idea of what was going on.

I did have the correct answer though.

These were experiences that would provide great journalistic material for those who would later sign my yearbook. There were also those solo acts, those self-generated feats that were sure to create lifelong memories for everyone who witnessed such things. Like when I had study hall in the auditorium.

I think it was around my junior year. The study hall was right after my lunch hour, and there should have been nothing that could go wrong. I could easily leave the cafeteria a few minutes early and roll on to the auditorium.

Brianna had the same study hall, and we usually were the first ones there, but the doors were always locked and the lights were out.

Usually, it was just Brianna and me waiting outside until one of the AV boys came to open up. We would then be the first ones in. The key holder was usually early or on time, but on that day he was late. Before long, everyone who had that study hall was congregated outside the door.

The herd was all gathered behind me. I knew they were there; I could hear them breathing. Their horns were sharpened, and their hoofs were ready to trample.

When the door was opened, I was eager to get inside, but the auditorium lights hadn't yet been turned on. The room was thick with darkness. I thought I'd be able to see well enough by the little light on my chair, but apparently not.

In my attempt to escape the crowd, I dropped the clutch, burnt some rubber, and ran full force into a knee wall in the back of the auditorium.

It was an incredibly hard knock. In fact, I hit so hard that my wheelchair did a near-180.

I was then facing the mob that I had so quickly tried to outrun.

Everyone laughed hysterically, including me.

Ella Wheeler Wilcox's poem *Solitude* says, *Laugh and the world laughs with you...*

I found it to be true that day. It didn't matter that they were laughing *at* me as much as they were laughing *with* me. I laugh at myself all the time, anyhow. (What can I say? Being me is just funny, sometimes. That's all there is to it.)

So, there we were. It was me and the world—at least my little corner of it—all laughing together, in synchronization and unity.

It has been said that music transcends all boundaries and can break through any barrier. Laughter does the same. In a split-second and by a single goofy act, the blockade was removed. Cohesive laughter crumbled the walls between us—if they ever really existed in the first place.

We were one, a whole unit, sharing the camaraderie of my own silliness, and it was amazingly pleasant. Guys and girls of varied cultures, ages, talents, and interests. Together we laughed like a band of dupes, joined in mindless solidarity.

But there was one kid who wasn't laughing; he looked genuinely concerned and asked if I was alright.

Obviously he didn't know I was a veteran. I had done that sort of thing before. The most memorable was in 3rd grade, when I had taken out nearly an entire row of desks.

It was one of those things that happened without knowing exactly how I managed to pull it off so well. I was sitting at my desk and had just finished a paper. I powered up my wheelchair, to turn in my work at the teacher's desk.

The kids who were seated in front of me had gotten up to turn in their work also.

It proved to be a good thing that their desks were empty because I didn't lower my chair enough and the joystick caught the underside of my desktop.

It just took off.

Instead of me driving the wheelchair, it was driving me...and my desk. I was merely a helpless passenger along for the ride. Against my will and the ability to prevent it, the controls were stuck at full-throttle, in the forward position.

Couldn't stop.

Couldn't steer.

Couldn't do anything, but ride it out.

I was like a Demolition Derby driver inside a factory showroom! There's a kid like that in every class. Wouldn't you know it would have to be me?

After jamming under my desk, my wheelchair became an Abrams tank. Thankfully, I didn't take any enemy fire.

Plowing onward and forging ahead, I rammed one desk into another, like the drunk driver had done at the red light a few years prior.

In a matter of no time, I had created an accordion of classroom furniture. Only after being overcome by the resistance of a large pile did my wheelchair finally come to a stop.

As it turned out, no one was hurt in the incident.

There was no serious damage.

No airbags deployed.

No points added to my driving record.

So, in the end, it turned out okay.

Now, here I was these many years later, demonstrating the same awesome driving abilities.

Of course I was alright; I was an experienced and certified crash test dummy. It was just too bad that I wasn't able to be graded on that.

23

Road Shows

It has been reported that most traffic accidents occur very close to the driver's home. The same can probably be said of motorized wheelchair crashes.

Surprisingly, I've had only one crash inside our house.

It occurred right after returning from school one day. As I made my way through the back door, the seat suddenly gave way and I took a quick plunge.

Mom always told me there would be days like that, but she never predicted that there would be so many of them. She never warned me that I'd have weeks that would consist of a string of Mondays, but I sometimes did.

Being born on that day, it may have just stuck with me.

Again I wasn't injured in the incident, and I was thankful that it happened at home, instead of at school. In reality, it gave the family one more thing to laugh about.

It also gave Dad one more thing to fix.

I'm convinced there would have been more in-home crashes if the construction of our house could have accommodated the size of my wheelchair.

Since it couldn't, I was forced to take my show on the road, thus impressing my friends with some of the aforementioned smashups on school property. Isn't that the reason our tax dollars go toward public education?

By taking my show on the road, it seemed fitting that I should also carry it into the street in front of our house, near the very land on which our taxes were paid.

It was there, on our street, during fair-weather season, that Brianna, Wade, Brandon, Cameron, and I would often play. Me in my wheelchair and them on their roller skates, I would gladly provide an exciting pull.

Free rides

Some things like that just beg to be tried by kids. Like a famous "double-dog dare" thrown down by the neighborhood tough guy, it just has to be done.

What could possibly go wrong, anyhow?

John Bunnell, former Sheriff and host of *World's Wildest Police Videos*, once said, "The quickest way to get hurt is to do something dumb."

He's a pretty smart guy.

And we were dumb kids.

My nieces and nephews would take turns holding onto a strap that they had connected to the back of my chair—and off we'd go.

That doesn't seem so dumb.

But we never went at a slow pace. They always wanted me to crank it up, and I was happy to do it. I'd fly up and down our hilly street, pulling them as fast as we could go. Of course the downhill direction was best for maximizing our speed…and our stupidity.

That'll leave a mark

For some reason, those excursions never ended without a serious scrape or two, or five.

One time in particular, it was Cameron who got the worst of it. We were blazing along, and maybe I zigged when I should have zagged. Or he might have gotten behind on his stopping efforts. As it turned out, he slammed directly into the back of me.

Technically, it was my second rear-end collision. Both occurred in my childhood, and both occurred close to home.

As we ground to a halt, I soon realized it was Cameron's leg that was doing all the grinding and halting. When I stopped, I discovered it was deeply lodged between my rear wheel and the wheel cover.

The poor kid was screaming to high heaven and quickly developing unresolved childhood issues in my very presences. I wasn't quite sure what to do about it.

That specific kind of circumstance wasn't mentioned in my operating manual. And having never taken any driver's education classes, the topic never came up as to how to respond to a human body part becoming embedded in my wheels.

Suddenly it had become quick-decision-making season, but I couldn't determine how to free him. I wasn't even sure just how he was stuck there.

It wasn't as if I was an expert on the intricate workings of the human leg or its potential suffering. Cameron's agonizing screams were of no real help either.

The whole thing was an unenviable position for both of us, in which we each had our own assignment; he felt the pain, I felt the panic.

Surely I didn't want to do anything to make the situation worse. By advanced instinct and sheer childhood brilliance, I realized panic was an adversary in such a predicament. I calmed down and began to think it through.

First, survey your surroundings and assess the immediate conditions. Check.

There was no approaching traffic.

No charging pit bull.

No stampeding herd of wild buffalo.

But there didn't seem to be any helpful resources at my disposal either.

Lowery's Law suggests, *If it jams, force it. If it breaks, it needed replacing anyway.*

Somehow I don' think Cameron would have appreciated me following that procedure or the logic behind it. The last thing our family needed was another kid with a piece missing.

As for replacement, if we could afford to do that, I probably would have had functioning prosthetic limbs of my own.

Nope, Lowery's Law was not a viable option.

Looking around further, I did see a man who was working near the top of a utility pole. I was sure he observed our dilemma. In fact, I believe I saw him watching, but he never came to help.

Looking back on it, I'm sure it wasn't feasible for him to climb down and assist us. But at the time, it added to my distress that he didn't offer to do that.

It was solely up to me to free my nephew.

I finally decided to move my wheelchair one way or another, but only slightly and slowly.

With a few subtle moves of my joystick, Cameron was finally free, and his screaming stopped. He acquired a good abrasion from the incident, but he endured it just fine.

No leg replacement was needed, but his did turn the most vibrant shades of purple that I've ever seen. Fortunately, he didn't require any medical treatment beyond the abilities of Nurse Janet, but the entire episode was scary and embarrassing.

Yet with things like this, I never wound up in traffic court, and none of my wrecks became part of any public record. If they had, I probably wouldn't have received the call to do an open driving demonstration at an outdoor community gathering.

It happened during the summer, when I was nine.

That was when I first discovered that the ringing of our telephone wasn't always a call from Doreen with another available foster baby.

One particular call was for me. Rather, it pertained to me. It came from Councilman Dilmore's office requesting my participation in the Volunteer Fireman's parade, which would be passing directly through our area.

First thought would be that they called because there was need of another clown. But if that were the case, they would have asked for Mom's help, especially if they'd want someone with the ability to toss candy to the crowd.

As it turned out, the event marked the Pittsburgh Port Authority's attainment of a new low-floor, rear-engine, wheelchair-accessible bus. It was the first of its kind in the county.

It was the new Kneeling bus, so named because the front rides lower than the rear, as if in a slight kneeling position. With features such as wide passenger entrances and no steps to climb, it was specifically designed for the infirm, elderly, or anyone with a physical disability.

The latest design of today's Kneeling bus allows it to also be tilted to the right side, to as low as curb height by the use of pneumatics or hydraulics, depending on the model. This makes wheelchair loading and unloading all the more convenient and much quicker.

The bus that I was asked to demonstrate was one that had a driver-operated mechanical lift. It was perfect for passengers like me, and apparently someone thought I was the right person to help introduce it to the local public.

If I accepted the invitation, my job was to demonstrate it on the parade route. My responsibility was to show the roadside audience how easily accessible it was for anyone in a wheelchair.

It all seemed simple enough; my role would be to roll.

But with such an unusual and unplanned request, there is the risk/reward ratio to be considered. Hence, another assessment was needed.

After all, wheelchairs are not always about fun and games.

I did realize there was some personal convenience built into the invite. The weather was quite warm and summery, which I have always favored, and I knew how to drive my wheelchair on and off a ramp or gangplank.

Also, the procession was within walking distance of our home. Then again, maybe that part wasn't so convenient, being in that magical proximity of where motorized accidents so often occur.

However, there wouldn't be any school desks to plow into or any nieces or nephews in tow on their roller skates…

Back and forth it went.

The reward of it was in the simple satisfaction that I'd be helping the city advertise the new bus that everyone was so excited about. For me, it seemed the Kneeling bus was tilted more toward risk than anything else.

I wasn't necessarily worried that I might steer into the path of an oncoming dump truck or drive into an open manhole, but I was concerned about doing everything just right, before countless pairs of watchful eyes. It seemed the blazing sun would become my personal spotlight, which is something that I felt uneasy about.

That was the true source of my apprehension—knowing parades were spectator events, and those spectators would consist of real living, breathing human people in my very own community.

There would be family, friends, and strangers of all ages, colors, shapes, and sizes. And they would all be looking at my every move. I didn't like the idea of being on display, having everyone gawking, scrutinizing, sizing me up. I'd much rather be under the radar than under a microscope.

If that weren't enough, the parade would also be covered by a local newspaper, *The Citizen*, who would specifically do an article about the Kneeling bus.

It all seemed a little overwhelming for a pint-sized nine-year-old. Despite my worries, I agreed to help out and do the demonstration.

I guess I didn't want to be the drip that would rain on their parade. I wanted their show to go on.

When the time came, Mom and Dad took me down to meet up with the bus. I got on, and the event began.

The parade route was lined with people standing or sitting on the sidewalks. So, the street itself would be the place where I'd make my exit and re-entrance. When the bus stopped at the first predetermined location, I knew it was my cue.

Show time!

Picture the imitation bird in an old German cuckoo clock. The door opens, the bird makes its appearance, it goes back in, and the door closes.

That was me, but at a slower pace.

Always at a slower pace.

I simply motored onto the ramp, and the bus driver lowered it. I then drove a short distance toward the sidewalk, as a narrator addressed the crowd and explained the features of the bus.

I'd then turned 180 degrees and drove back onto the bus. The driver raised the ramp, and we moved further on with the parade.

There was really nothing to it.

The idea was to simply show the Kneeling bus to the community, not to impress anyone with my driving skills or entertain them with my crashing abilities. So, I remained focused on the true agenda.

That was the whole trick—to concentrate on my task and ignore the crowd. And that was my only trick; I didn't do anything fancy.

No bleach burnouts.

No wheelies.

No doughnuts.

We then proceeded to the next stop and repeated the process. It was over after a few stops. By concentrating solely on my driving duties, I don't even know how the crowd responded or what their expressions were.

As it turned out, everything went very well and according to plan. My only embarrassment was that I was being watched by everyone and that *The Citizen* ran an article about the bus and about my involvement in the demonstration. The piece included a picture of me in my wheelchair driving onto the ramp.

Who would have thought that a new bus and a girl in a wheelchair would create a baseline of media attention? People often refer to such exposure as their fifteen minutes of fame. For me, that's fifteen minutes too much. But at least the parade concluded with no additional close-to-home accidents to be added to my list of driving mishaps.

In all, it was a good day. The best part was that, like Cameron's street ordeal, I survived it just fine—minus the purple tread marks on human skin.

24

Sweet Renovations

Any venture out had the potential of becoming an adventure for me. Whether playing in the street during summer break or motoring off to school, life always found a way to keep me on my toes—figuratively speaking of course.

As you can probably already tell, school was a particular challenge. At day's end, it was home, sweet home. I was always glad to return there, even if I hadn't been left stranded in a hallway or didn't crash into any walls.

Afterwards, I didn't go for pizza with friends or hang at the local video arcade. I didn't roam the neighborhood or prowl the city streets.

Furthermore, in spite of my attraction to paints and my appreciation for art, I never went out to paint the town red. For one thing, it would have clashed with the color schemes of our professional sports teams here. Plus, I simply had no time for extracurricular activities or after-school delinquencies.

As it was, my days were long. Sometimes my evenings seemed longer. On a typical school day, I was up at six o'clock. Never a serious breakfast person, my entire morning was dedicated to personal beautification efforts.

Some of us require more work than others.

This became more extensive and meticulous when I turned thirteen and was permitted by Mom to wear makeup. I must admit, however, I sometimes tried to sneak a little eyeliner and mascara when I started seventh grade. I figured it was close enough to my thirteenth birthday that I could get away with it.

Mom always caught me though.

It's funny that she has always had trouble remembering exactly when my birthday was, but she knew I hadn't had it yet.

Consequently, makeup would not be legalized until then.

In the daily grind of my usual routine, I rolled onto the bus at seven. School began at eight. It was a marked achievement to make it to my first class on time, but being such a stickler for punctuality, I can honestly say I was never late.

After a day of learning the lessons and acquiring any necessary bumps and bruises, I boarded the bus again at three o'clock. I knew a mountain of homework lay ahead because I was dragging it home with me.

It was the sequel to my school day.

I am someone who is hip-deep in carpet fiber when standing on my bedroom floor. At my size, molehills become mountains. So, it seems appropriate to compare my stack of homework to one. When I returned home, I immediately began confronting that mountain.

Normal stuff, basically.

Standard practice for a regular school kid.

It was my need to create unusual methods and modified procedures that made doing homework so cumbersome and time-consuming, but it was all I had to work with.

It began with a nose dove into my book bag to drag everything out. I had to be careful to not leave any bite marks, so it wouldn't look like the dog tried to eat my homework.

As for writing, I've always been obsessed about maintaining immaculate penmanship. If my papers weren't written perfectly, I rewrote them. That probably goes back to when I was little and hated to color outside the lines.

I also liked to get everything done before bedtime, so I wouldn't have to rely on study hall the next day. That's not to say I never had homework to finish in study hall; I just always aimed to get it done the night before to eliminate the worry of it.

We never knew when there'd be an impromptu assembly or one of those inconvenient fire drills, but there was a good chance something would happen during my study hall, on a day when my homework wasn't finished. Or we'd probably have a category five hurricane show up out of nowhere and knock the power out.

I didn't like taking any chances because I felt the odds wouldn't be in my favor. So, I was sure to apply myself at home as much as in class.

Taking a break was particularly beneficial, especially when I was really tired or when my back was hurting. My homework halftime consisted of dinner and a shower. After that, it was back to the books.

Reading has always taken me longer than most people because it seems that my brain transponder is often set at a five-minute delay. It's not that I'm a slow reader; I'm a fast reader with slow comprehension. The contents often passed me like a military flyover.

Having not understood the material, I'd have to read it all over again. It didn't help matters that I'm also a slow page turner. Some people thumb through pages with ease; I lip through them, kissing one page at a time.

It's my own form of lip reading.

Typically, it would be eight o'clock or later by the time I finished my homework. I'd try to turn in by nine, so I could attain adequate rest to get up and go do it all over again the next day.

That was my routine, and those were my procedures. I'm used to having to improvise. I'm quite proficient at it, but my tasks still requires more time than most people.

Compared to the average citizen, I'll always be the one-legged turtle in a cross-country race, no matter how skilled I've become.

That's okay though. I'm in no hurry.

My life was always as normal as possible. This is what my parents wanted for me, and I am blessed because of it and so much better off.

Having no hands or feet was no reason for them to wait on me, hand and foot.

I've always done as much as I could on my own, no matter how many tries were necessary and regardless of how long it took. Of course, I have also had help with things that I hadn't mastered.

For example: Mom threaded the needle of the sewing machine, but I learned to operate it okay. The foot pedal became a hip pedal, and the endpoints of my arms were great for guiding the material. I've never sewn a zipper onto my arm or given myself sutures in the process.

Any such accomplishment has been a victory for me because the doctors had said I'd never do anything. They insisted I'd pine away, strapped in a chair, drooling into a cup.

Well, they never said anything about drool; I just threw that in to add some theatrics.

Regardless, my parents didn't accept their prognosis. There would be no pining on their watch. That would have been equivalent to putting me in a room and not feeding me, as was initially suggested.

I had a life to live, and I'd live it as normal as everyone else in the Brooks family–if you want to call them normal.

We are a family unit. Yet, we are all individuals, as were each link in the chain of foster babies who passed through our home.

As individuals, we all have needs to fill and interests to pursue. I'm no different. I just had to engage a bit of creativity. Being vertically challenged requires some lateral thinking, and I have found that we can grab hold of life just fine without hands.

For me there has been a great deal of trial and error. A little ingenuity and patience goes a long way. It has helped me to lead an ordinary life with somewhat-adequate independence.

Yet, I have discovered a sweet paradox in this.

There have come numerous occurrences that have lovingly challenged my claim to normalcy. They have delicately confronted the intricacies of my existence without infringing upon my will or crossing the border of favoritism.

Basically, that's a poetic way of saying I've always tried to accomplish things on my own, and no one could teach me how to do it or how to improve my methods—that was all up to me. Yet, others have taken it upon themselves to make improvements that have greatly eased my limitations.

Those efforts surpassed the temporary limbs, the powered wheelchair, and the special desk at school. Significant alterations have been made to our home as well.

These projects spanned several years, and they were done exclusively on my behalf. In fact, if I gave you the nickel tour, you'd probably think I completely rule the place.

It began by adding the ramp to the back porch, where I loved playing when I was little. That feature provided easy entrance, but there would also come interior improvements that offered me some additional conveniences.

Whether doing the work himself or hiring it out, Dad was always the initiator, overseer, and chief inspector of these projects. Of his measured words and rationed verbiage, he has often said, "Some people have to work around here."

If he has a favorite saying, it's probably that. First he'd say it, and then he'd demonstrate it by going off to work or by carrying out some kind of home improvement activity.

The most prominent and practical among these is an addition that was built when I was about eleven. While I was anticipating the thrill of legally wearing makeup, my family was considering much larger things that I'd appreciate. One of those was actually a much needed amenity.

Dad, Brian, and Noah performed most of the grunt work. It began with a big dig, manually removing sod and soil to create an extended foundation alongside the house. They then cut and removed an arrangement of blocks from the basement wall.

Mark Hubert took over from there.

The project wasn't a man cave for the boys or an expanded workshop for Dad; it was my own custom bathroom, a world-class tinkletorium!

What woman doesn't want one of those? Maybe it was a tradeoff for not having a large and expensive gathering of footwear.

It wasn't as if I needed a big walk-in closet or expanded storage for my unlimited handbag collection. A practical, user-friendly bathroom was ideal.

In terms of convenience, this bathroom was topnotch, but at a lower level of course. Everything was appropriately shrunken, sunken, or somehow modified specifically for my needs.

Normally, kids start out on a small potty and graduate to the full-size luxury model, with all the elaborate features such as a hinged seat and swirling water.

I actually needed to downsize with everything.

If an aerial view was available, it would probably look like any other bathroom with the exception of the toilet water, which happens to swirl clockwise.

Some people have claimed that it's supposed to swirl counterclockwise in the northern hemisphere. However, this notion has been debunked by others as nothing more than a myth, and I think I can support the debunkers on that one. Or maybe it's just another example of how things are different in my world.

Swirling water aside, I live at ground level. From there my bathroom looks nothing like the one that I had always been used to. Like in the movie *Elf*, to me, our toilet was "ginormous."

It's not that it loomed over me like Pittsburgh's U.S. Steel Tower; I'm actually a few inches taller than a standard toilet's overall height. But it's still too big for me in a practical sense. Mom always had to lift me onto it.

With my new personal, customized unit, she wouldn't have to do that. Our reenactment had ended; we'd no longer be planting the flag on Iwo Jima, whenever I'd have to go.

My new commode and sink were the standard type, but each was sunk into the floor for easy access. My bathtub was made of fiberglass, manufactured by a local boat company. It too was recessed flush to the floor, and it had molded steps on the inside that allowed me to step down into it. For the most part, I could also operate the sink and bathtub faucets with my little arms.

Eventually my parents had the first bathtub replaced with a regular above-floor, walk-in model because they were concerned I might slip or stumble on the steps as I outgrew their size. The walk-in tub came from Florida, which gives me another reason to love the place, but that's getting a little ahead of myself.

The entire bathroom project took only about two months, at most, from the time Dad and the boys first poked a shovel into the dirt to when the final piece of trim was nailed in place.

The venture was so successful that another soon followed. That too was done on my behalf.

As a kid, I was the town crier. I liked watching everything from the front porch, offering play-by-play commentary on who was doing what. I often called out to Mom to let her know who was coming, who was going, whose dog was on the loose, et cetera.

It kept me occupied and offered cheap entertainment.

At my parent's request, Mark followed the bathroom build with a living room project, where he removed the front wall and extended it over the front porch. He then installed five floor-length windows, so I'd be able to see out and continue my neighborhood watch reports from inside the house.

That was really nice during the winter months.

There was yet another great "Amy amenity" brought into our home, which significantly enhanced my quality of life. It was a wonderful add-on, but it wasn't a home expansion project. The supplementary convenience of which I speak was an indoor stair lift.

That particular feature had come along a few years earlier, when I was about ten. It also came with a bundle of humor, as if it was included in the packaging.

This contraption proved to be a great help to me and a small hazard for others, Mom especially.

The unit is pretty basic, but it has been very reliable over the years, with little maintenance required. What a priceless value it was that I'd no longer have to scramble up the steps to go to bed!

No more grappling hooks, carabineers, or pick axes needed!

Before enjoying my smooth ascent with a panoramic view of the staircase, someone first had to lift me onto the seat because the track ended just above floor level. This left the seat elevated enough that I couldn't climb onto it by myself.

After a few years of that, Dad designed modifications for it. He drew up plans to have the track extended at the bottom. This included the installation of a trapdoor that would accept the extra track and allow the seat to stop flush to the floor.

After planning it out, Dad took the idea to the company who built and installed the lift, and they came out and made the requested modifications.

I'm no mechanical major or electrical engineer, but it basically worked like this: I'd no longer have to be lifted onto the seat, but someone had to manually open the trapdoor at the foot of the stairs.

A push of a small button would bring my chair down from its lower home position, which was just a few steps up. When the bottom portion of the chair settled into the opening in the floor, I climbed aboard. Another push of the button took me to the summit where the chair remained flush at the top.

Going back down was the reverse process, but after I climbed off the chair, the button would take it back up those few steps to allow the trapdoor to be closed.

The thing worked great.

Dad is brilliant!

Mom...not so much.

The only inherent danger with my chairlift came after the modifications, if the trapdoor was left open. That happened on a few occasions.

One night, after everyone had gone to bed, Mom stayed up to finish watching a television show. This meant she was the only person downstairs.

After I went up, Dad yelled down to Mom, "Don't forget the trapdoor's open."

"Yeah, I know," she muttered. "Don't worry; I'll get it."

Did she really have to be reminded like a six-year-old?

Soon after, Mom turned off the television. She then turned off the light and proceeded to step directly into the dark abyss at the bottom of the stairs.

The seat to my chairlift is pretty small, as is the hole that receives it. Though Mom is a thin woman, she insists her measurements exceed that of the opening. Somehow, she managed to fill it, like a round peg in a square hole.

It was an extremely tight fit, but she fit, nonetheless.

I heard the "thump" but nothing else. No one called for help, so I figured everything was fine. Apparently, the others were all asleep by then, and Mom was left to fend for herself. Luckily, her survival instincts kicked in.

It was the embarrassing thought of having to be extricated by the fire department that gave her the sheer will to pull herself to safely. Plus, she certainly didn't want Dad to know that she was stuck in a rabbit hole.

He had warned her, after all.

Mom wiggled and squirmed, and after straining to maintain her ladylike dignity, she was eventually able to free herself and hobble off to bed in disgust.

If the whole thing had been videotaped, it would have surely gone viral on the Internet. Since that wasn't the case, she appeared to have gotten away with it. She endured it under the cover of darkness, and none of us would be the wiser.

During the wee morning hours, Myia awoke to find Mom in the hallway. She was on her way to the bathroom, crawling on all fours.

When Myia asked what was wrong, the first thing Mom could think to say was that she was pretending to be Bob Dog—the floppy, howling character on *Mister Rodgers' Neighborhood*.

As it turned out, she had three broken bones in her foot.

There'd be no hiding that from Dad.

Concerning my stair lift, I guess one girl's upgrade is another girl's foot trauma, but I'm glad to say Mom did make a full recovery.

In all—though they now have become somewhat antiquated—the room expansion, the bathroom, and the lift have proven to be great investments in my wellbeing. And the laughable thought of Bob Dog have made our home that much sweeter.

25

Keepers of Amy

Besides those in and around our home, there have been other special friends, casual acquaintances, and near-strangers who have helped look out for me at times. I'm thankful for each of them, no matter how seemingly insignificant their deeds.

Appearing in all forms, several of these individuals were obvious culprits, and others were the least likely of suspects. Most notable were some that I encountered at school.

As every school has its share of jokers, pranksters, and limbless students in reckless wheelchairs, there seems to be a brutal, unwritten rule somewhere that school just wouldn't be official without a bully or two. There was at least one of those at Northgate.

No, it wasn't me.

Despite my left cross and laser guided spitting abilities, bullying just wasn't my thing. If it were, I knew I wouldn't have gotten the job had I applied for it because the spot was already filled.

The boy who held the title and wore the championship belt in heavyweight bullying seemed to fit the part very well. He was rude and crude and certainly didn't appear any too friendly, which is probably what helped him secure the bully position.

I certainly didn't want to cross the guy, and I hardly ever did because he wasn't at school very often. Though I never saw him actually rough up anyone, he seemed perfectly capable of doing it. He just had that air about him, that intimidating presence, as someone who'd probably have to tie a pork chop around his neck to even get a dog to go near him.

The guy's attitude and language suggested that he was someone to steer clear of. If there was anyone in school that I'd run into—literally—I didn't want it to be him.

It would have been a hit-and-run for sure.

In time, however, I discovered there was something unexpectedly different about that guy. Not only did he never direct any bother or bullying in my direction, he actually seemed to look out for me.

If he noticed me coming up the sidewalk, he opened the door. If he saw me trying to make my way through the thick pipeline of students, he squeezed ahead to create a clear path. I never really interacted with him, but it was great that this bully would display such a caring side.

When everyone laughed at my crash into the auditorium wall, he was the one who didn't laugh. He was the kid who inquired of my well-being. It was him, the school bully, who expressed some real concern for my safety.

As mentioned earlier, Noah was good at looking out for me, in school as well as at home. Of my siblings, he and I are closest in age. Still, there's an eight-year age gap between us that I haven't yet been able to fill, even with my wheelchair set on high speed.

When I was in grade school at Avalon Elementary, Noah was in high school at Northgate. During his junior and senior years, which would have been third and fourth grades for me, Noah scheduled his study halls to correspond with my gym class.

With the two schools barely a mile apart, Mom specifically permitted Noah to use the car on my gym days, so he could come and interact with me.

I greatly appreciated him doing that because I just wasn't much into volleyball or rope climbing. However, I did participate in one of the regular gym class activities: I could hang from the rings really well.

Our gym teacher, Mr. Allen, would lift me up, and I'd grab the rings under my little arms and hold on as long as I could.

I remember being the one to hang there the longest.

So, for those who are keeping score, I could execute a stair-falling dismount and hang from the rings. To this day, I don't know why I didn't pursue a career as a gymnast.

Regardless, I liked having Noah come to my gym class. If he couldn't make it, I'd walk back and forth across the gymnasium for exercise. More often than not though, Noah would come and play ball with me while the other kids had gym class. And we actually had a real ball instead of him using me for one like Myia had done.

Sometimes Noah would roll a basketball to me, and I'd roll it back. He would also toss a little plastic ball, which I caught by trapping it between my chin and shoulder. I'd then throw it back with a quick fling from my shoulder and little arm.

Noah taught me how to do things like that. All the while, he kept his eyes and ears open to be sure no one gave me a hard time or caused me any problems.

When Noah graduated and was no longer around, my nephew, Brandon, seemed to take over that roll, addressing any behind-the-scenes problems and behind-my-back issues.

Of course, Brianna looked out for me—being a friend as well as my niece. She walked me to class when possible, and she even rode the short bus with me for a few years, so she could help me with my coat.

Along with Emily, there was Kate and Beth, although Beth's first name is actually Sarah, and that's what we called her back then. She now goes by Beth, which I'm quite partial to as far as middle names go.

I believe it was my senior year when Kate and Beth would accompany me from lunch to English class. Again, we arrived early. The room was empty, and we'd sit in there by ourselves.

For fun, Beth would read the first and last lines from portions of a book titled *Falling Up*, by Shel Silverstein.

For example: there's a poem in the book that reads,

> *We gave you a chance*
> *To water the plants*
> *We didn't mean that way*
> *Now zip up your pants*

Beth's abbreviated rendering would read:

> *We gave you a chance*
> *Now zip up your pants*

These poems were funny as they were but putting the lines together like that was hysterical—and we'd just laugh like fools. Sometimes Beth would engage her intellectual side and try to analyze the poems for some deeper meaning or hidden symbolism.

I've known Beth for practically my entire life, and we have been close since grade school. She lived near our home, and her grandmother actually made me my first coat.

It was during the time when I wore the banana arm, which made it extremely difficult for Mom to get coats on me. So, Beth's grandmother, Mrs. Keener, made me a hooded cape. It fit well, and it kept me warm.

A big "thank you" to Mrs. Keener is well-fitting, as I reflect upon my friendship with her amusing granddaughter.

I didn't meet Kate until high school, but she has been a true friend. She and Beth were artsy and talented. They usually stole the spotlight in the school plays.

One year I played the grandmother in *Willie Wonka And The Chocolate Factory*. I sat in my wheelchair "sewing" a blanket.

Though I may have had one or two speaking lines, the rest were left to the pros like Kate and Beth. They are widely remembered for their outstanding performances, but I cherish the many personal memories that I shared with them off stage.

Mrs. Myers will always have a special place in my heart. Each of the aforementioned and various other faculty and friends have offered assistance and extended generosity, far beyond the acceptable range.

All are Grade-A, Number One, USDA approved–keepers of Amy.

Surpassing all recommended standards, they have greatly exceeded the minimum dosage of human compassion and the daily allowance of personal kindness. However, these do not complete the list of those who have been an utmost blessing to me.

The earlier chapters strongly illustrate the startling reality that I encountered with entering an intimidating high school building. That year—seventh grade—was the hardest of times, but it proved to be the greatest of times as well.

This was due to the efforts of my science teacher, Mrs. Glencer. As science teachers go, she was as good as any and better than most. As a humanitarian, she was amazing.

Mrs. Glencer was the mastermind and guilty party behind an astounding act of benevolence on my behalf. She conceptualized the details and implemented the plan with military precision and composed perfection.

I didn't ask for it, didn't expect it, and never saw it coming.

But it happened, and Mrs. Glencer was the chief culprit.

Her idea was sparked during *Be Kind to Animals Week*. In the course of that time, an annual school assembly was conducted by the Humane Society. Mrs. Glencer then had a private discussion with my mom and decided she wanted to do something to help me.

Before you start laughing, I must quickly add that it was not as if Mrs. Glencer viewed me as a member of the animal kingdom, where kindness should be bestowed upon me as such; she just felt inspired to employ the use of a loving, well-trained animal to provide me practical, everyday assistance.

At Mrs. Glencer's urging, and with her guidance, my seventh grade class organized a fundraiser that involved selling Sarris chocolate bars.

Even now, I feel honored, and I remain grateful to them and to everyone in the Pittsburgh area who had a craving for fine chocolate and for their willingness to spend a dollar or more to acquire it.

26

Girl's Best Friend

A sweet soul, a sweet tooth, and a thin dollar bill.

That's all it would take, many times over, to hit the target.

A strategy was devised, and the footwork was set in motion. It all began door-to-door and with the stopping of innocent passers-by. Anyone who looked like they had a dollar became a potential customer.

The project started in May and continued throughout the final few weeks of the school year. The transaction consisted of trading various delicious Sarris chocolate bars, in exchange for American currency bearing the image of President George Washington.

An assortment of pocket change equaling that amount was just as accepted. It was so easy a seventh grader could do it, and they did it, rigorously.

I'd have to think there might have been a direct correlation between the amount of candy bars sold and the number of new cases of tooth decay in the area. Though there were no published reports to confirm this belief, simple reasoning would apply because sales were through the roof.

Mrs. Glencer also contacted the media, and the story ran in *The Citizen* and *The Pittsburgh Post-Gazette*. From there, it took off like crazy.

News readers began sending donations. Those contributions were many, and they were generous.

The goal set by Mrs. Glencer was clear and specific, and it would be fully achieved. The plan was to raise money to buy me a service dog!

I was thankful that the earlier home improvement activities had taken place for me, and I couldn't have imagined anything more.

Now this!

Everyone in the school seemed excited about participating in the fundraiser, but I didn't understand the full magnitude of it at the time. While researching and communicating with former classmates for the purpose of writing this book, I came to realize that it was all much bigger than I had known.

As I look back on it with the detailed information and newly obtained insight, two of the newspaper's pre-sale photos appear a bit prophetic.

In one picture, Dana is seated next to me, which was highly appropriate; she was my closest friend back then. She also went on to be the absolute highest seller. Directly behind me in the other photo was a boy named Ken. He ended up being the second highest seller.

The astonishing thing with Ken is that he and I had never spoken to each other. He was always occupied with getting into trouble—much like Noah but at a deeper level—and I was always occupied with ignoring him because of it.

The fundraising kit contained thirty chocolate bars per box. Having a good product was of utmost significance. Having a good location was too.

Ken's mom worked at a local food store. So, Ken and his cousin, Karyn, camped out in front of the place, selling four or five boxes a week.

Looking back, Ken was another of those bully types who had a softer heart than his exterior had revealed. Upon learning of his contribution, these many years later, I thanked him.

In response, Ken simply claimed, "It was my one good deed in a high school career otherwise plagued with detentions, suspensions, and other various unruliness."

It truly was a good deed. And being so well-spoken about it, he apparently received a decent education in spite of his other behaviors.

Prior to the time of the candy sale, Ken was often removed from class for a variety of wrongdoings. During the sale, he was once removed for a different reason: Mrs. Glencer pulled him and Karyn aside to update them on the sales numbers because they were such heavy hitters.

In fact, she proudly informed them that they were runners-up. Nobody was able to touch Dana's numbers, but after her, Ken and Karyn thumped everyone.

While it's impossible to mention all who were involved, another notable contributor was Rich Books. His family lived just a few streets over from us, and he and I had been classmates all throughout school.

Although his dad's name is also Richard, they are no relation to us. Apparently, the postal service thought otherwise and assumed we all lived together, as Richard's mail was often delivered to our house.

In the candy selling process, Rich set out on foot, and he even approached neighbors he didn't like and people he preferred to not encounter. He did that for me, and those people purchased chocolate bars from him on my behalf.

Clearly, the aim of the candy selling fundraising effort was spot-on. When they eyed the target, they pierced it, dead center. In fact, the arrow passed through and continued further than anyone had anticipated.

I never knew how much money was raised in the short lifespan of the fundraiser, but it was sufficient enough to purchase the dog, paid-in-full. There was even a surplus, which would cover vet bills and dog food for an entire year!

As the Brooks' home was always open to numerous foster babies, it was also never without a dog or two, and I was well-acquainted with these fine creatures.

I have to admit that monkeys have always been my favorite animal, but dogs are true companions. They are unquestionably loyal and trustworthy.

Service dogs, in particular, are amazing. They are intelligent and specifically trained for the exact needs of their owner.

Because of this, taking possession of such an animal is no quick or easy procedure. They don't arrive as a catalog selection or an off-the-rack purchase. There is nothing generic about them, and there is nothing random or haphazard in their training process.

My dog would be purchased through "PAWS With A Cause," located in Wayland, Michigan. After a complete assessment of my diagnosis and living condition, the organization would choose from the best suited canine candidates and begin training them for my specific needs.

At least two dogs that I know of had gone through the specialized training on my behalf. Shortly before graduating from the course, both were eventually disqualified for one reason or another.

Each failure began the process all over again.

One of the dogs failed while being introduced to travel and to the general public on a shopping trip because it growled and snarled at all the men it encountered.

Back to the selection pool.

After a full two-year ordeal, a final replacement had been trained, but even that success had come with a slice of amusing drama.

These dogs are in constant human contact, learning vocal commands from their trainer. Therefore, they are previously named by the PAWS organization. My dog came with a small glitch concerning this detail.

During the training of my dog, we were informed that she had been named Janet. Mom said we couldn't have two dogs in the house with the same name. We probably would have had way too much fun with that.

As a result, one of them would have to be renamed. Though the dog had both a head and a tail, Mom was sure to win the coin flip.

The folks at PAWS stated that we should rename my dog something reasonable—a name closely resembling the one that she had already known. Because she had green eyes, someone suggested Jade as an alternative.

I liked it.

Jade it was.

By the time she completed her training, she had adjusted to her new name, and we were ready to be formally introduced.

In May of my freshman year, my very own service dog was delivered to our home. Jade arrived with her trainer, Gerry.

A pleasant gentleman and PAWS volunteer, Gerry had been the head trainer of military dogs with the Army, guarding missile sites during the Vietnam War.

Jade was a Golden Retriever/Labrador mix, which was comparable to me owning a horse because her back came to about the top of my shoulder.

She had just turned two years old the month prior, and her weight was in the neighborhood of 85 pounds. Though she was completely paid for, she had also come with a sticker price of somewhere around $8,500.

If your non-metric algebra agrees with mine, that would be about a hundred bucks per pound of doggie weight. That was several years ago. Nowadays these extraordinary animals cost much more.

In 2011, a woman was arrested for stealing a service dog that had been trained for a child with Cerebral Palsy. The dog's value was estimated at $20,000. What makes that story especially disturbing is that it happened here in the Pittsburgh area.

Fortunately, that particular dog was recovered, but others have not been so lucky. Many trained service dogs have been stolen and sold. Others have been maliciously killed.

When Jade and Gerry arrived at our home, Mom, Dad, Noah, and I were there to greet them. The dog strolled in with pride and confidence, as if she knew this was to be her new home. Though I was excited to finally have her, my first thought was one of vanity.

Her fur was actually more a caramel-blonde than gold, which was okay. It was the dog's nose that stuck out to me.

Well…of course it would stick out; she wasn't a Pug, after all. It's just that her actual nose was the same color as her fur. It wasn't black like other dogs, and I couldn't help but think she looked funny because of it.

To be fair, she might have thought I looked funny too—not so much because my nose was the same color as the rest of me, but maybe because I was the only human in the room who was void of solid hair color. Mine had streaks of blonde highlights.

If Jade was bothered by that, she didn't let on. She came over and plopped down next to me with perfect contentment.

Gerry then filled us in with the other details.

Jade had completed her offsite training, but we would have to go through a bonding process and joint training before she would become certified and permitted to go into public with me.

For her it was like a soldier who had graduated from boot camp and was now in need of advanced specialized training. I think that would be a good analogy. You'd have to ask my dad about that stuff to verify it.

When Gerry left our house, thunder rumbled in the distance, and we noticed a Pittsburgh storm was brewing. Jade noticed it too. She immediately hopped onto the couch and hunkered down.

That wasn't going to set well in our home, with Mom and Dad especially. She wasn't there on sabbatical. She wasn't there as a pampered guest or privileged visitor. She was supposed to be a working girl, not a stuffed animal or a throw pillow.

Gerry had scarcely pulled away from the curb when the follies began. Try as we might, we couldn't get Jade to obey our commands to vacate her position on the couch.

We told her, "Down! Down!"

She didn't move.

We continued. "Down! Down! Get down! Jade, get down!"

The dog still didn't budge.

So, we said it louder. "Down! Down!"

It didn't do any good. She just lay there looking at us as if we weren't even speaking her language.

Well, you know what I mean.

We took turns, "Down! Get down!"

Was she a trained service dog or a small mule in a costume?

She just wouldn't listen.

We were then forced to use drastic measures; we consulted the printed guide that Gerry had given us. When all else fails, read the instructions, right?

We quickly discovered Jade was smarter than we initially thought. It was no wonder that she wasn't responding to "down." She was already doing it; she was lying *down*.

When we said "off," she immediately hopped off the couch.

Silly humans!

We were glad to finally figure out the proper command, and it was good that Jade followed it, but it wouldn't help with the fact that she was skittish of thunderstorms. I remembered what that was like; I too was afraid of them when I was a kid.

I don't think either of us slept much our first night together. For me, it wasn't because of the storm. As it all began to sink in, I was just so excited and thankful to finally have Jade.

Up to that day, she had only been a promise, a letter of intent. She was an unseen animal in an unknown town. Now she had become a reality. She was mine, free and clear.

My excitement was also blended with a streak of worry.

Jade would bunk in my room from the first night on, but she had to sleep in her crate for about a week while she acclimated to her new surroundings. I lay awake worrying that she was uncomfortable in there.

Eventually, I'd come to realize that she liked sleeping in that thing. In no time, I'd also discover this funny looking dog would become my best friend and my "beautiful lady."

My Jadey lady

27

Shattered Glass

A rut has been described by some as "a grave with both ends kicked out."

To be stuck there isn't necessarily pleasant. Ruts are often steep and muddy, and if you're in one, you're probably in it alone. They offer no tour guides or illuminated exit signs—and finding your way out may seem hopeless.

If that's an accurate depiction of a rut, it might be said that a routine is more like a long-running, fragile glass tube. It presents a smoother, clearer, less resistant corridor in which to travel. As we follow it, we walk the straight and narrow and focus on what's in front of us. This helps us to avoid wandering off and becoming lost.

I realize routines are predictable and possibly boring to some, but there is often comfort and safety within their rhythmic flow.

Each page of the calendar is nearly identical, as are the days that are printed on them. Everything is very commonplace. Everything is quite normal. That is, until someone throws an object and shatters it—such as a paper folder, for example.

That's what happened one day when I returned home from school, shortly after receiving Jade.

By that time, I thought everything was beginning to level out. Our home had received returned visits from stringers and photographers from the newspapers, and they ran follow-up stories on Jade and me, showing where the candy sales and the donated funds had gone.

As before, I felt a little embarrassed by all the attention. But Jade didn't seem to mind it when she was included.

After the stories ran, I assumed life would get back to normal. I figured I'd finish out the remaining few days of my freshman year and enjoy the summer with Jade.

I recalled how, two years prior, much of my summer break was dedicated to writing "thank you" notes to those who sent checks for the fundraiser, and I was happy to do it. Now I was able to tangibly experience Jade's presence and completely appreciate her company.

Though I'd be making the abrupt transition from school year attendance to summertime absenteeism, it was all part of the routine. The only real difference was that Jade was now with me.

She and I were bonding well, and she was becoming more beautiful to me each day. We were also scheduled to meet with Gerry on specific summer weekends for our team training.

That was all I was anticipating at the time. I expected nothing else. For Jade and me, it seemed that only the "dog days" of summer lay ahead. Routine was beginning to reemerge, and everything was as it should be.

That was when the glass tube shattered.

It happened because of another event that had been secretly in the making.

I came home from school that day to find Mom acting quietly giddy. Something was up.

Of course with her that wasn't particularly out of the ordinary. She had sleeves, and there was often something up them. That was part of her own routine, I suppose.

This was different, though.

Mom placed a homemade folder on the table in front of me and urged me to read through it. When I opened the folder, I immediately recognized Mom's handwriting.

In big, proud letters she had written, *We are going to Disney World!*

As with my homework, it didn't take me long to read it. Also, as with my homework, I didn't get it. It didn't sink in. I recognized the words, but my comprehension seemed to perform another military flyover.

First off, who do you mean by "we"?

Secondly, why are you going there?

Were Mom and Dad taking a sabbatical from all the foster work? Were they leaving Jade to completely look after me? If I had fingers, I would have been scratching my forehead in bewilderment.

And then, with a long, one-sentence, breathless explanation, Mom proceeded to enlighten me. Or at least she attempted to. She started going on about information she had received from her friend, Sally—about the Make-A-Wish Foundation and how they grant wishes to kids who are considered disabled or terminally ill.

(Sadly and ironically, Miss Sally passed away during the writing of this very part of my book. She suffered a terminally illness of her own, which she kept concealed. Her death came as an unexpected shock to us, but I think she'd be glad to know she is missed and that we mentioned her in this chapter.)

Given the Make-A-Wish information, Mom was typical *"Mom."* She thought such an extravagant opportunity should go to a more deserving family, possibly someone battling a terminal disease.

In the grand scheme of things, I suppose we are all terminal, but the sad reality is that there were young kids who were badly afflicted and facing untimely death. Mom felt they should be the ones going to Disney World, not us.

That was the demon she wrestled when submitting my application. The determining factor was that we probably wouldn't be selected anyhow because of the other more worthy candidates.

Though she was reluctant to do so, Mom had filled out the paperwork. The application required references, and Dr. Alexander was among the first of them. He had no reluctance, whatsoever.

Mom mailed the form without further consideration. Much to her surprise, a Make-A-Wish representative came to the house to interview her and Dad. Everything took place while I was in school, leaving me completely clueless.

Two months after the application was mailed, I sat there gawking at those words inside the folder, as Mom spilled the details. I listened as best I could while excitedly looking over the contents of the folder.

The pockets were stuffed with brochures, Make-A-Wish literature, and Disney information, along with airline tickets, vouchers, and coupons.

I just couldn't believe it.

Obviously, it took me awhile to get what Mom was saying.

"*We*" meant "*us.*"

The trip was because of me, and I'd be going too!

My daily routine had been shattered, and it was a breaking that was joyously welcomed. Best of all, it left no jagged shards behind for anyone to step on.

28

Elevated Concerns

Often in life, upturns come with a downside. If mine had any, it was that I was unable to take Jade on the Disney trip because we hadn't undergone our team training, and she wasn't certified.

Also, the intense heat and high humidity wouldn't have been good for her. It probably isn't good for anyone, but I was happy to go sample it. I just hated to leave Jade.

The poor dog was probably confused by everything. She had been transplanted from Michigan to our home in Pennsylvania. A month later, we would leave her there with Candy and the foster babies, so we can jet off to Florida.

It was highly likely that Jade never made the geographical connections, noted the timelines, or mapped the travel routes, but she was aware of the changes. She knew we were leaving without her. I felt sad to have to do that. It was the only bitterness sprinkled into the pot of honey.

That isn't to say everything else went off without a hitch or that there were no other concerns along the way. We did experience some obstacles of various proportions and at different levels.

Noah drove us to the airport and saw us off. It was Mom, Dad, Myia, Cameron, and me. I was fifteen years old and had never been inside an airport. I didn't have any worries about it; I understood the concept and the primary function of the place. It was the security measures that surprised me.

This was long before 2001 and the 9-11 tragedy, but I seemed to heighten the suspicions and concerns of every badge-wearing person in the entire airport.

After the baggage and everything was checked, I was thoroughly inspected. Though I am little in body mass and there isn't much to analyze, they examined me like a suspicious, unattended package.

Fortunately, the National Guards weren't called in, and I didn't have to submit to an FBI interrogation or an NTSB inquiry.

To expedite the process, they probably should have just placed me on the conveyer and ran me through the x-ray machine like a carryon.

After checking me all over, they also wanted to remove the battery from my wheelchair. My parents had to explain that they were just gel batteries and said they couldn't take them out.

Content with the information, Security finally turned the chair over to the baggage handlers who treated it like any other piece of luggage. This is a fair assumption because they would eventually return it to us damaged.

As for me, I was ferried to my seat with first-class limousine service. Well…I was actually placed onto a luggage gurney and wheeled aboard, which was quite embarrassing. I felt like a refrigerator being wheeled aboard a cargo plane to be delivered to its destination.

Of course, I'd be a mini-fridge, not a full-size unit. I'd also probably go as a bargain-rate, scratch-and-dent item because of the car accident. (Though it had been nearly ten years, only the outer scratches had healed; the internal dents remained.)

Cameron, Myia, and I were all first-time flyers. We rookies sat together on one side of the aisle while Mom and Dad sat on the other. Cameron was as excited as I was to be on an airplane. He chose the window seat.

I sat closest to the aisle for an easier exit, in case anything happened. That left Myia in the middle. For Cameron and me, it was exhilarating to be venturing into the vast skies above us.

Being of such low center of gravity, I think I valued it more than the others.

Myia was scared out of her wits. For some reason, she didn't find much comfort in being book-ended by her scrawny seven-year-old child and her limbless sister. So, she took some Dramamine to calm her nerves and settle her stomach.

After taking off and leveling at cruising altitude, Cameron seemed a bit puzzled. Peering out the window, he finally asked why the states weren't in different colors like they were on the maps he had seen at school.

I didn't expect the ground to be color-coded, but it would have been nice if someone had put dotted lines around the state borders or posted a few tall markers to inform air travelers of their flying position.

Myia had her own concerns. She wouldn't have known what color the states were because she was too afraid to open her eyes, much less peek out the window. Purple, pink, orange, or blue, it didn't matter; she just wanted to return to Earth.

You'd think for being such a sun junkie, she'd appreciate being six miles closer to it.

Apparently not.

Added to her problems was the Dramamine. It seemed she took too much of it, and the stuff really wasn't agreeing with her. Or maybe it was overly agreeing. Whatever the explanation, it made her quite loopy.

As her luck would have it, she also had to use the bathroom during the flight. When she got up and began to amble up the aisle, Mom couldn't pass the opportunity to tease her. She told Myia that she should sit back down because she could make the plane tilt.

Loopy or not, Myia knew enough to realize Mom was only joking. It probably came automatically from years of exposure. She laughed it off and proceeded to the bathroom, but we would learn later that she didn't recall any of it.

If I had to guess, I'd say the only thing Myia remembered of the entire flight was that "in the event of a water landing your seat cushion can be used as a floatation device." It was a theory that went untested, however, and she was probably glad about that.

A short time later, the plane did tilt, but Myia had nothing to do with it; the pilots were credited with that, as they dipped the nose forward and descended upon Orlando.

To my delight, there were no border agents present to elect whether or not to grant me entrance into the state. This meant I wouldn't have to be searched, screened, or further scrutinized—not until it was time to leave, anyhow.

After all the other passengers had deplaned, another luggage gurney appeared, and I was placed upon it for my sophisticated disembarkment.

The mini-fudge had arrived.

Scratch-and-dent girl was soon reunited with her scratch-and-dent wheelchair. Needless to say, we were disappointed to discover the damage. A button cover was missing and would remain so, and the joystick wasn't working properly. I'm not sure what the problem was with that, but Dad was able to somehow get it working again.

Even on vacation, his mechanical know-how and problem-solving talents were accessible. It was a good thing we had brought him along. Dad always seemed to make it so there was one less thing to worry about.

Fixing Myia would be another thing. Only time and sleep would do that.

29

Wish Trip

B ags claimed, heads counted, and all loose items gathered, we soon
located a man from Make-A-Wish who was holding up a sign for
us. He presented Dad with a key to the van that we'd be using
during our stay, and we were on our own—headed for a week of fun in
the sun!

Upon exiting the man-made, air-conditioned airport environment, I
received my first introduction to a tropical climate. It extremely contrasted
the place we had departed two hours earlier.

Wheels-up from Pittsburgh, the temperature was only in the '60s.
I knew it would be much warmer in Florida, but I didn't expect every
thermometer to be pegged to their limits. Nor did I anticipate the stifling
90% humidity.

Boiling temperatures and drinkable air—you gotta love that, right?
As atmospherically shocking as it was, I was delighted beyond words to be
there.

I really appreciated seeing palm trees growing in their natural setting,
compared to the one Mom had standing in the old pot in our living room.
For some reason, I didn't feel the need to taste one like I did as a toddler.

Our first order of business was to get settled into the little village house that we were provided. Nestled among other such units in the Disney village outside the theme parks, it was to be our new temporary home.

The place was adorable and just being there was fun.

We immediately began to unpack. While taking inventory of our belongings and deciding where everything should go, we noticed something was missing besides my button cover.

The good news was that we were confident it wasn't left on the plane or lost by the baggage handlers. It was there a few minutes ago. We figured it might be a good idea to find it because this thing that went missing was actually a person.

Of course, you could assume it would be the rambunctious seven-year-old boy who'd wander off, but it wasn't—it was his mom who had disappeared.

Looking around, we discovered Myia face down on a bed like a drunken sailor. Later, she remembered nothing after taking the Dramamine at Pittsburgh International Airport, until waking up in the village house in central Florida.

The village itself was amazing and extremely cute.

With a swimming pool, merry-go-round, restaurant, and a play area, the place was a vacation spot onto itself. For the duration of our stay, the name on our street sign had been changed to *"Amy Street."* I've been thinking about having that done in Pittsburgh, but I haven't acted upon it yet.

As an added perk, it seemed our village house also came with family pet readiness because we encountered a friendly stray cat our first day there. It was right outside our window, looking in at us.

By that time, Myia had awakened from her Dramamine stupor. When she saw the cat, she opened one of the Lunchables from the stocked refrigerator and started feeding him.

Mom told her to stop doing that, but she and Dad had to attend a meeting in the village. While they were away, we continued our feline feeding activities.

When we heard Mom and Dad returning, we hurried away from the cat and pretended to have been watching television the whole time.

As they read this book, hopefully my parents will doze off before getting to that part, so we won't get into trouble for that.

Another "pet" that welcomed us was in the form of a black snake. We found it slithering near the wheel of the van as we were getting ready to go out. It was so tiny and cute, but also a tough little thing.

We were afraid of it because its head was held up like a cobra, ready to strike, and we didn't know if it was poisonous or not. One of the village workers soon appeared and tossed it into the adjoining wooded area.

There are also the tiny lizards that run around everywhere. I had never seen them run free like that. Cameron and I made it our mission to catch one.

Me in my wheelchair and Cameron on foot, we chased those little guys all over the place but never caught a single lizard. It was fun to try though.

By the way, don't believe everything you see on television; not a single one of them spoke or attempted to save us money on car insurance.

All non-speaking reptiles aside, there is of course the main attraction—the magical theme parks. Appropriately positioned in the middle of the state, Walt Disney World seems to represent the very heart of Florida. And the extreme heat of it.

Being our first trip there, none of us could adapt well to the temperatures. For the first couple of days, we were physically miserable. Forget the notion that "a lady never sweats, she only perspires."

I sweated like a woolly beast.

At that time I'd love to have been a refrigerator. Not a mini-fridge, but a massive side-by-side with ice-maker included. Florida can certainly use a few more of those, and the bigger the better. There should be one on every corner, with doors flung open, running at full capacity.

I love being warm, but the last thing I wanted was to shrivel to a smaller dress size. I remember going through the parks and sweating so much that I'd have to remove my prosthetic arms and pour out the sweat. Appealing, huh?

Dad probably should have used his pocket knife to cut off the fingertips, allowing them to drain naturally.

Due to the unbearable heat, we missed a lot of the great things that Disney had to offer. We found ourselves dodging sun drops as best we could by skipping many open attractions and darting from one air-conditioned spot to another.

Sweat and all, I fell in love with the place. We all did.

It really changed the way we viewed vacationing.

With me being in a wheelchair, we all got moved to the front of the lines at the theme parks. More than that, I loved that I could be included on almost every ride in one way or another. Some even allowed me to remain in my wheelchair.

That was unusual for me.

I was used to being carried onto the rides at Idlewild—a theme park we often visited in Ligonier, Pennsylvania. Ride restrictions were another issue that I often faced, but those problems were very scarce at Disney.

Whichever park we attended there, we usually left around four to get dinner on our way back to the village. Every day, upon our return, Cameron and I would have gifts and treats waiting for us somewhere in the house—courtesy of Make-A-Wish.

Cameron would always race to the door and ask if he could use the keycard to open it because he just had to be the first one inside. When the week was all over, Dad would be the last one out because he had to lock up. None of us wanted to leave.

With the sunburns, the heat rash, and the mild dehydration, Make-A-Wish had given us the trip of a lifetime. As a result, Walt Disney World has become my favorite vacation spot, and Florida has become my favorite state.

Contrasting the massive attractions is a simplicity that abides there: summer means flip-flops, winter means flip-flops with socks. The only way it could possibly be any easier is if you don't have feet.

As for Walt Disney World, it appears to be quite a Mickey Mouse organization. And wonderfully so!

30

Small World

Some say the earth is round, and I tend to agree. Living in the rugged pitches and deep valleys of Pittsburgh, I knew it wasn't flat. I've also believed that if you're my size and hadn't really been anywhere, the world as a whole is a rather large place. That was the case when I was selected for the Disney trip.

For the first fifteen years of my life, I had never done any traveling, except for a few land excursions to Wilmington, Delaware. Even then, we drove the straightest route possible.

No one seemed to mind us taking a shortcut through a portion of Maryland to get there. So apparently, we weren't trespassing or violating any popular travel laws.

Aside from that, I had always been landlocked in Pennsylvania and tethered to Pittsburgh, in particular. That was okay with me. Other than the short-lived teenaged shyness, I had always been comfortable with myself and content with the world in which I lived.

Don't get me wrong; I desired to travel. I wanted to go places, see things, and do stuff, but my inner fulfillment wasn't contingent upon that. I was content with or without doing those things.

French novelist Marcel Proust said, "The real voyage of discovery consists, not in seeking new landscapes, but in having new eyes."

I could always relate to that. Maybe it's because I have a creative imagination and artistic vision.

Of course, if we'd like a less stylish rendering of the concept of such serenity, we can draw upon the wisdom of an old Cajun philosopher, who once said, "Be what you is."

It didn't matter that I was the needle in the haystack or just another pebble in the quarry. I was satisfied being myself. I was happy being a "mini-me."

A "Who down in Whoville" or a "Munchkin in the land of Oz." If that's who I is, I'm fine with that. I've lived my life accordingly. I truly had no complaints, especially after receiving Jade.

All was well.

Even Myia faired better on the return trip and ingested much less Dramamine than she did on the out-flight. I felt grateful for all of it.

So, the Disney trip arrived as an amazing and unexpected bonus, and it passed as a joyous and unforgettable adventure. It was an exception to the rule that if something sounds too good to be true, it probably is.

The people at Make-A-Wish and the entire Disney family cut no corners and spared no expense. Before the plane landed and the dust settled, it left me wondering why I should be blessed with such a gift.

At 30,000 feet or so, the flight had attempted to confirm my earlier suspicions that the world was a massive place. But when the trip was all over, I wasn't so sure.

Disney's Epcot represents inhabitants of varied cultures located under one invisible roof. To visit there is to visit everywhere and at different expanses of time. It erases neighboring borders and eliminates boundaries of faraway lands, mixing and compressing all of civilization into one.

Maybe that's why the states weren't color-coded or traced with dotted lines. I'd venture to say other countries aren't either. Could it be God's way of telling us that we are all to live as a united people?

Yet, I am only one—a small one—among the masses.

Make-A-Wish chose me, regardless. Somehow, they found me, and they selected me above so many others who probably should have gone instead.

Why me?

How did they find such a little person on such a large planet?

Having done so, I have no doubt that the Make-A-Wish Foundation could have also located my missing button cover had I asked them to because, apparently, it really is a small world after all.

31

Of Dogs and Men

Having endured my Greek lesson earlier, how about something from the English dialect of the Lowlands of Scotland?

Here's a sample for you:

The best laid schemes o' mice an' men gang aft agley.

That's a quote from the 1785 Scot's poem, *To A Mouse*, by Robert Burns.

The Standard English translation says it more clearly:

The best laid schemes of mice and men often go awry.

I have to admit I'm no expert on mice or their scheming abilities, mainly because Mom has always kept a tidy enough house that we've never had a rodent problem.

Hospital clean, military tight.

Regardless, I do understand the concept of this famous line—how things we devise often lack the intended outcome or the most favorable results. This can be predominantly true if you substitute the mice for one caramel-colored Labrador named Jade.

That was my experience.

After taking in the thrill of long-range tourism and the entire Disney adventure, we came home a bit sun baked and sky worn. But I was as excited to return as I had been to leave because Jade was waiting for me, and I was eager to see her.

Following the unexpected 824-mile detour to Orlando and back again, our summer schedule immediately got on track. From there, everything appeared to be going as planned.

The best laid schemes of dogs and men proceeded without further interruption. But there seemed to be a fine line between the unfolding of those plans and the complete unraveling of them. We somehow found that balancing point and managed to teeter upon it.

When Gerry delivered Jade and she hunkered down on our couch, we had no idea at the time of just how telling her actions were. Jade was visibly shaken by the rumbling of the distant thunder, but we could not have known if it was a temporary response to the uncertainty of being transported to our home or if there was a deeper issue.

Only time would reveal that.

Other things were revealed sooner.

A segment of Jade's early training with PAWS included learning how to cover and uncover someone in bed. That was something specific to my needs, and her trainers were sure to add it to the repertoire.

However, it came with a hidden flaw.

Jade was trained using a regular bed of standard size and of the usual arrangement—a mattress over a box spring on a typical bed frame.

For easy access, my bed merely consists of a mattress on my bedroom floor. It is also positioned ninety degrees to the wall, meaning I sleep crossways.

These practical details created a few wrinkles with my bed coverings.

No pun intended.

Well…maybe a little.

Jade was perfectly capable of pulling my covers up or down. Like any command she was given, she did it enthusiastically, with tail wagging and with a gleam of pride in her lively green eyes.

It was the bed's height and configuration that complicated matters for her. This in turn created some discomforts for me. Instead of walking around the bed to pull the covers from one side at a time, Jade simply stepped onto it and trampled me.

Squashing my stuffing out was not in anyone's plans, mine especially. I soon realized I simply couldn't utilize Jade's talents for that specific routine, which was something that had always been a struggle for me.

Covering was always difficult, but sometimes the real struggle develops under the cloak of darkness. I toss and turn a lot at night, the effects of which are not fully realized until the sun appears.

That's when I'd often awaken like a tightly rolled burrito and would have to reenact a Harry Houdini straightjacket escape in order to free myself.

Jade could offer no practical assistance with that. Instead, she became a one-member audience who witnessed my morning escapes.

After we completed our joint training, which spanned the entire summer, Gerry cleared us to venture out with Jade into the real world. Her duties would be basic, but her presence was greatly valued. I was proud to have her with me, and others were pleased to meet her.

Most people love dogs, or they at least appreciate a friendly encounter with them. Jade offered that. Additionally, I discovered that the more attention Jade received, the less people noticed anything different about me. That was unquestionably the greatest benefit of her accompanying me in public.

Oftentimes with Jade at my side, people didn't even seem to notice me at all. I liked that. It greatly served my community shyness.

In spite of the few wheelchair mishaps I've had and my willingness to laugh about them, I never really was the proverbial bull in a china shop. Then again, Mom knew better than to ever take me into a china shop. But she did often take me shopping, and Jade joined us initially.

With her I could roam off from Mom to another part of the store to look around and not have to worry because Jade was there to pick things up for me.

She wasn't taught to lap up a spill in aisle five, and she never had to do that. But if my purse dropped from the arm of my wheelchair, Jade gladly picked it up.

One thing Jade was specifically trained for and expected to do was attend school with me. That was something that didn't work out so well.

She had been trained to lie under the seat of my wheelchair, under the desk. But because it happened that my seat had once given way, we were afraid of that happening again, crushing Jade beneath me.

As an alternative, we considered having her lie beside me in the aisle. However, that could have created a trip hazard as the other students would be forced to step over her. And being in the open, there would also be the temptation for the kids to pet her and play with her.

Our final determination was that Jade would be at risk of being disturbed and the class would be susceptible to distraction. So, we decided she would not attend school with me as planned.

When I went off to school that September, it was like leaving for Disney World all over again, in that Jade just hated to see me go, and I hated to leave her behind.

Early on, Jade and I had become very close. She followed me everywhere, which was effortless on her part. Even on my best days, I was always easy to keep up with. As I would sit on the floor in front of the couch, Jade would squeeze in and lie behind me.

This served a dual purpose; it fulfilled the bodily warmth that Jade seemed to enjoy, and it offered support to my lower back. Ultimately, her body pressure helped alleviate some of the persistent back pain that I've had since the car accident.

I valued that, and I enjoyed it. Mom would often disclose how much Jade missed me throughout the school day, and it saddened me to know that it saddened her.

Sometimes after I'd leave, Jade would go and sit close to Mom. She would then give her a paw to hold, and Mom would hold it. It wasn't a daily routine of theirs, only when Jade demonstrated that specific need. It seemed to make her feel better, and Mom didn't mind.

Jade knew that she belonged to me. She understood that she was there to help satisfy my needs. And she did what she could for me around the house—picking things up from the floor, turning lights on and off, opening and closing doors.

Having escorted me at other times, she seemed lost as to why she couldn't go off to school with me as well. It was heartbreaking for both of us.

Finally, I don't recall if it was my junior or senior year, but on the last day of school I decided to take Jade with me and allow her to make an appearance. It was the most fitting time as any since there wouldn't be much work or anything on that day.

Though she wasn't required to do so, Mom called the school the day before to let them know. It was a courtesy thing, not an obligation because Jade was legally allowed to accompany me anywhere in public—including a *public* school.

Apparently someone didn't get the memo.

When Jade and I arrived the next day, we were quickly greeted with opposition.

At least I was.

Though I'm not sure if it was the principal or the vice principal, the man asked me why I had brought a dog into the school.

I was quite stunned by that.

However, he might have thought that it was some sort of an end-of-the-year prank.

I explained that Jade was my service dog and that my mom had called the day before to let the school board know that I'd be bringing her.

He didn't seem all that convinced or impressed, but he let us proceed anyway.

Later, as I was making my rounds, I told Mrs. Glencer about the encounter, and she became like a woman scorned. I don't know if she had targeted the right person or not, but she marched straight to the office where she confronted the principal and boldly explained to him that Jade had just as much right to be in the school as he did, if not more.

Shortly thereafter, I was invited to take Jade down to the administration's office to show off her skills to the superintendent.

There was a small room full of faculty assembled there, and they received Jade and me quite warmly, which was possibly a result of all the heat that had been blown at them by Mrs. Glencer.

I decided to have Jade demonstrate how she could pick up a sheet of paper from the floor. Of course she showboated. Instead of just picking up the paper, she had to pounce on it and kill it first.

At day's end, all was well with Jade accompanying me to school. I was happy that we were able to share the experience together, if only on that one occasion.

As time went on, we realized that Jade was truly and deeply afraid of thunderstorms. I had gotten over that. I had outgrown it. But Jade didn't; she worsened. My worry of storms had diminished to the rudimentary concern that Mom or Dad wouldn't come in to close my bedroom window before the rain came in.

With Jade, however, her weather fears were much more intense. Upon this discovery and with observing her worsening fears, Jade could no longer go into public with me as originally intended.

So, whether you're citing Burns or Brooks, the simple fact remains: *The best laid schemes o' dogs an' men gang aft agley.*

32

Crayolas and Monkey Business

There's No Business Like Show Business

That's an old song by Irving Berlin.

Of course, this is not to imply that there are any *new* songs by him. No disrespect intended for a man who is regarded as one of the greatest songwriters in the history of our nation, but everything associated with him is old by now.

Even he was 101 when he passed.

A person can acquire a lot of information over such a prodigious span of time. With his escalating knowledge, Mr. Berlin apparently learned a thing or two about show business, enough that he committed some of it to song.

Myself, I prefer monkey business.

If Mom is part Florence Nightingale, I am part Jane Goodall. Though I loved Jade, I have always completely adored monkeys.

For as long as I can remember, monkeys have held the title of being my favorite animal, though I'm not sure why I so easily gravitated toward them. It was probably because they are just so cute and fun to watch.

I've always appreciated the details of their facial expressions and how they show such emotion. They are also the only animal capable of truly wrapping their arms around you, and they do so with the right motives and for the same reasons that we do.

As if I need to further justify my love for Florida, it was there that I received my first good measure of primate exposure, on what was our forth visit to the Sunshine State.

Each of our previous southern vacations had included Disney World and a variation of accompanying family members. On our last trip, it was only Mom, Dad, and me, and we decided to mix things up and do something completely different.

No offense to Mickey and Minnie and friends, but we chose to bypass Disney and drive straight to Boca Raton to visit Mom's friend, Rosa. It was then that I got to see the Atlantic Ocean for the first time.

After a week and a half at Rosa's place, we then traveled down to Miami. Rosa accompanied us and proudly showed us around like a professional tour guide.

Along the way, I couldn't help but notice how all the houses were so individually and brightly colored—much more so there in Miami than in the Orlando area. It reminded me of my 64-count box of Crayola crayons that I had as a kid.

Back then I greatly enjoyed my coloring books and crayons. It was a big deal to me to always have the biggest box of crayons that was available.

The more colors, the better.

I not only tended to use as many colors as I could—even if it was unrealistic for the picture—I also blended them, tint upon tint, tone upon tone, one shade upon another. I mixed and matched and blended and swirled as if to create colors that had never before been discovered by the human eye.

Imagine what I could have done with today's 120-count box!

It's funny that I was always so stringent about not going outside the lines, but when it came to color patterns, I broke every rule known to man and beast alike.

One particular monkey could attest to this.

It wasn't a real monkey; it was one that I had created on paper as an art project in junior high school.

The assignment called for working in complimentary colors. I chose to draw an abstract monkey, which I then proceeded to color orange and blue.

As it turned out, my art teacher, Mrs. Massucci, nominated me and that effervescent monkey for some sort of award, which I subsequently won. I was then featured in the *Pittsburgh Post-Gazette* for it.

Mrs. Massucci also wanted me to take additional art courses after completing my mandatory class, but I foolishly declined.

Though I did outgrow my use of crayons, I still love colors, and Miami was alive with them. One specific area of it was also alive with monkeys.

It's a 30-acre wildlife park called Monkey Jungle.

Knowing my fascination for those of the monkey kingdom, Mom, Dad, and Rosa made it their strictest priority to take me there.

The place is an incredible establishment, the business of which is about nothing but monkeys! And they were all basically running loose—just roaming all over—as if they own the place!

The tagline of Monkey Jungle states: *Where the humans are caged and the monkeys run wild.*

Considering the people we sometimes encounter, that actually could be a good idea for everyday life.

At Monkey Jungle it already is their everyday life. Guests simply walk among the monkeys by passing through a series of tunnel cages.

The place is a monkey-lover's paradise.

It's a monkey haven.

And a monkey heaven.

I vividly recall how badly I wanted to bring one of the inhabitants home with us. I believe it was a spider monkey. The thing got so close that it seemed we could have easily scooped it up and smuggled it out of there.

I'd have to think that there might be some kind of law against that. Or I could have gladly just stayed with them, but the monkeys probably wouldn't have me.

I also remember when I was very young and how I pleaded with my parents to buy me a real monkey. Having begged and bugged them relentlessly, Mom said I could have one for my sixteenth birthday.

When that day came, there was no monkey. There was none in a gift bag, none in a box, and none with a ribbon or bow.

For one thing, Mom never thought I would have remembered her telling me I could have one, but I did. Kids just don't forget things like that.

As it turned out, my parents had truly considered buying me one to assist me around the house. Why use monkey arms if you could have a whole monkey, right?

Owning one would have been practical for getting items that were slightly out of my reach and perfect for climbing up to the objects that were completely inaccessible to me.

It would have also saved me a lot of going up and down the stairs and from room to room for basic goods, and I'm sure it could have been trained to do my bedcovers without using me for a mini trampoline.

There was a time when I had taken it upon myself to research and contact an organization called Helping Hands, where they trained capuchins for quadriplegics. After completing the first and second stages of the interview process, they stopped answering my calls.

It was probably for the best anyway. There was a reason why Mom and Dad had decided against the idea of me owing a monkey. Major considerations were of the inherent safety risks.

Monkeys can be moody and unpredictable. If it ever decided to turn on me, for whatever reason, I wouldn't be able to properly defend myself against an attack. My face and throat would be left virtually unprotected.

With this knowledge, my parents decided the risk/reward ratio was not in my favor. There would be no "Dunston" checking in with us.

As a young girl, I was given a stuffed white monkey that had long arms and Velcro hands. I often walked around the house with him wrapped around my neck in a relentless hug.

I also had a stuffed baby gorilla with a pacifier. I didn't name the gorilla, but I called the monkey Charlie, though it wasn't for reasons that some might suspect. I named him as a compliment, after the man from church who gave him to me.

It might have been equally appropriate if I had named him after Charles Darwin, but I suppose that would have been an insult—as much to the stuffed monkey as to the man.

I still have Charlie and the nameless gorilla. Both are safely tucked inside a box in the attic.

To this day, I admire primates of all types—real and manufactured, colored, or stuffed.

I've just never bought the idea that humans have emerged from them. If we did, I have to wonder why monkeys have not continued to evolve into humans.

We still have monkeys.

We still have humans.

Neither have changed or replaced each other. We are separate and distinct with nothing in between.

Simply stated, I am a person, not a primate.

To Mr. Darwin, I can only say, *Sorry, Charlie.*

It's interesting that we can travel the entire world and only discover three different types of rocks, but Monkey Jungle holds thirty different species of primates in one isolated area. Among that assortment, which totaled about four hundred, I didn't see a single one that was somewhere between man and monkey.

Unfortunately, I also didn't see any of the abstract variety or ones that were hand colored orange and blue.

It left me wondering, *Where's my box of crayons?*

33

Graduation Speech

Also apparent is that a rumor is true. As Mom stated, I did graduate high school as an Honors student.

Thankfully, they don't make you give a speech for being one of those. Of the student body, only the class Valedictorian and Salutatorian does that.

Regular Honors students are basically no different than the class clowns in that all are required to stay seated and remain silent. Being accustomed to sitting and preferring to be quiet, those were pleasant conditions for me.

Yep, I had certainly changed a lot since verbally chewing the ear of a van driver while nibbling Happy Meals.

Thus, I certainly would *not* have desired to deliver a commencement speech to "my fellow graduates, family, friends, faculty, staff, and honored guests."

I wouldn't even want to do that for the behind-the-scenes people such as the custodian or the lady at the lunch counter.

That was one of the reasons I was so reluctant to write a book. Granted, it isn't the same as appearing before an audience of what would consist of about a gazillion intimidating faces.

Writing a manuscript in the privacy of your home is nothing in comparison to giving a live speech in real time, to real-life, breathing people individuals of the human variety. Yet, I am speaking to an audience, regardless.

There remains an element of risk and a splash of trepidation either way. As for you readers, each of you are a one-at-a-time audience. So, whether spoken or printed, it would only be fitting to offer something with take-home value—no homework assignments or cluttering handout sheets though.

And no test at the end of the chapter.

I don't have to even worry about doing my make-up or fixing my hair because the good thing is that I'm not on stage, sweating beneath a glaring spotlight. I have no notes to shuffle. I don't have to sip water or clear my throat.

Best of all, I'm not forced to enact the age-old trick of picturing everyone in their underwear to settle my nerves.

Those common obstacles being non-factors, I'd have to consider what "school of thought" I could leave with you if I were to submit a commencement speech in written form. I suppose it would be something like this:

My Graduation Speech

My dear friends, in 976 words or less, I'd like to divulge my secret of becoming an Honors student, in spite of the grueling workload and physical exertion.

To do that, I must begin by humbly spelling out a cold, hard fact:

I am S~M~R~T

That doesn't sound very convincing, does it?

Well, what If I said that I'm at least way more brighter than all the other Brooks kids?

Still doesn't cut it, huh?

Okay, to be completely truthful, I can tell you that I'm nowhere near as intelligent as either of my brothers. So, let's move from the ridiculous to the realistic, shall we?

How about a quote?

Let's take this one for a test drive ~

"Ninety percent of life is showing up"

Feel free to jot that down in case you want to use it sometime. I really won't mind. It isn't my saying, anyhow; actor Woody Allen coined it.

Though mathematical statistics and numerical calculations were not my absolute favorite ~ with all those numbers and integers and such ~ I want to offer that particular citation. As it is, someone had to go to the trouble of determining that percentage, so I think it should be put to good use.

Also, the axiom is true.

Showing up is the hardest part.

That's the worst of it.

Show up!

That requirement often appears in multiple forms. It probably will mean different things to different people at different times.

Though it is a task that isn't necessarily easy to fulfill, we must show up. Doing so is vital to reaching any anticipated level of success.

Show up for family.

Show up for school.

Show up for work.

Show up for life.

Period.

In that secret lies the majority of any worthwhile accomplishment.

That's it.

The rest is simply carrying out our duties ~ doing what is expected of us.

Those are the things I did.

I showed up.

I did my work.

With that, nothing was handed to me. I wouldn't have been able to reach out and accept it anyhow. I received good grades because I earned them, but not by doing anything exceptional.

Just showing up and completing my work.

No evening classes.

No tutoring sessions.

No extra credit or special assignments.

I didn't cut any corners either.

Seldom absent.

Never late.

I showed up.

90%

Though the quote belongs to Mr. Allen, I learned the practice of that concept from others. Among them, I have to thank my teachers. I've always had good ones and not only in the classroom.

It began with my parents.

They have always led by example.

They have always taught by doing.

Without fail, Mom and Dad showed up.

They were there for each other.

They were there for us kids.

They were there for the scores of foster babies.

My parents ~ I knew they had my back, no matter what. Never were they parental helicopters hovering over my shoulder, but they did perform frequent flyovers to make sure I had whatever I needed.

As far as percentages go, their total is 110%

You see, commitment and dependability go a long, long way. You might be surprised at what you can learn or accomplish if you simply show up and do what's expected of you.

To do that, you may have to discover better ways to do things, as I have had to do. Sometimes you have to invent them. That's been the story of my life, of which I am now sharing a portion with you.

I had to figure out how to do my schoolwork ~ everything from opening my book bag to developing good penmanship.

For me, this was all part of showing up besides just being in class.

At home, for me "showing up" meant many things, including sneezing a lot when dusting with a Swiffer in my mouth. Or having to apply a rear naked choke hold to use a shop vac.

Don't worry: that isn't as bad as it might sound. It's actually a legitimate martial arts maneuver.

And then comes the extremely essential tasks of life such as sending text messages. I have a friend in Ohio who has two perfectly good texting thumbs. He insists that I am merely faking it about not having hands because he claims that I text faster than he does. Though I sometimes use my arm for that ~ like I do on my computer keyboard ~ I mostly text with my bare mouth because I discovered that's what works best for me.

When I do so, I guess you could say that each message I send is sealed with a kiss. Consider it a bonus. But your bonus to yourself and to others is to show up.

Unfortunately, we live in a civilization that often wants to invest the least amount of effort and magically reap the maximum gain. We want to squeak by, by the skin of our teeth.

I might be missing some fleshy parts, but I'm quite sure the human tooth doesn't even have skin.

Squeaking by doesn't work; we must show up in full.

If I may throw in another quotation at no additional charge, it would come at the courtesy of Mr. Thomas Alva Edison, who said, "There is no substitute for hard work."

Corner cutting is not a good drive path to success.

Quick fixes rarely hold together.

We have to show up.

We have to do what needs to be done.

Without me ever imagining any of you in your underwear, consider that my message today ~ show up.

Whatever your status, whatever your title, whatever your position or aspiration ~ show up.

Clock in.
Do your work.
Carry it to completion.
Don't compromise quality.
I promise you won't regret it. You can all trust me on this.
After all, I am an Honors student, remember?
I'm a Jenius with a capital J!

Me with my parents, Rich and Janet, to whom I dedicate this book.

Acknowledgments

Thanks goes, above all, to my Lord and Savior, Jesus Christ. To Him be all the glory. Thank you to my parents, Rich and Janet, for living a Godly example before me and shaping me into the God-fearing woman that I am today.

To my brothers and sisters, Brian, Candy, Myia and Noah, for accepting me fully as their littlest sister and never thinking of me as anything less.

To Dr. Michael Alexander for being the first doctor to believe in me.

Thank you to the crew at *Pine Valley Chiropractic*, Dr. Brian Green, Dr. Michael Cole, Dr. Bob Stover, Miss Becky, and Miss Mary, for not being afraid to try new things for the betterment of my health. You have become like a second family to me.

From *Wholistic Acupuncture and Natural Medicine,* Miss Sydnie Bryant L.Ac. You are such a blessing to me in so many ways.

Thanks to the *Band of Brothers* for always being there when a new project comes up.

Thank you, Eric, for always believing in me, especially when I don't believe in myself. You push me out of my comfort zone to be a better "me," and I am forever grateful for your continual encouragement.

To my friends, Jen, Matt, Todd, and Ulf, for always being there. You are true friends that lift me up when I am down and rejoice with me in my triumphs.

Thank you to Pastor Jeff Leake of *Allison Park Assembly of God*, for teaching God's word in such an applicable way. I leave service every week wanting more of Jesus.

To Mr. John Paul Owles, president and publisher of *Joshua Tree Publishing*, I am forever grateful.

Last, but not least, thank you to Jeff Ferris for putting up with my antics for the last 2 1/2 years, and to his wife, Miss Ginny, for graciously allowing me to intrude on their time together. Jeff, you have selflessly poured yourself into this project and gave no less than 100%. I am so proud of the end product, and I'm in prayerful anticipation of the adventures God has in store for all involved.

CPSIA information can be obtained at www.ICGtesting.com
Printed in the USA
BVOW02s2242290415

397700BV00003B/3/P